POLICY ANALYSIS

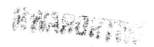

THOMAS R. DYE

POLICY
ANALYSIS

WHAT GOVERNMENTS DO,
WHY THEY DO IT,
AND
WHAT DIFFERENCE IT MAKES

THE UNIVERSITY OF ALABAMA PRESS

University, Alabama

Library of Congress Cataloging in Publication Data

Dye, Thomas R
Policy analysis.

Includes index.
1. Policy sciences.   I. Title.
H61.D94   300′.1   75-37717
ISBN 0-8173-4834-4 (hardback)
ISBN 0-8173-4835-2 (paperback)

CONTENTS

361.61
D995p

ACKNOWLEDGMENTS

I am grateful to the Southern Regional Training Program in Public Administration for the opportunity to develop my ideas regarding the state of contemporary public policy research in a series of lectures at the University of Alabama in 1974. These lectures enbled me to discuss problems in policy analysis which I have encountered directly in my own research and indirectly in my attempts to understand the work of others. These lectures devlop in more detail several themes which were introduced at the undergraduate level in *Understanding Public Policy*, 2nd ed. (Englewood Cliffs, New Jersey: Prentice Hall, 1975).

I am especially appreciative of the support of Professors Coleman B. Ransone Jr., Robert Highsaw, and Donald Strong at the University of Alabama, who have contributed so much over the years to the enrichment of public administration and political science in the Southern region.

1 PUBLIC POLICY AND SOCIAL SCIENCE: KNOWLEDGE AND ACTION

Policy Analysis and Political Science

Policy analysis is finding out what governments do, why they do it, and what difference it makes. More elaborate definitions of policy analysis can be found in the academic literature. But they really boil down to the same thing—the description and explanation of the causes and consequences of government activity.

Public policy is whatever governments chose to do or not to do. Some scholars claim to see a difference between specific government actions and overall programs of action toward a given goal. They insist that government action must have goal in order to be labeled "policy." But all we can really observe is what governments choose to do or not to do. So realistically, our notion of public policy must include all actions of government—not just the stated intentions of governments or public officials.

Governments do many things—in national defense, foreign relations, education, welfare, health, the environment, police protection, transportation, housing, urban development, taxing, spending, and so on. Indeed simply finding out what

1

goverments are doing in so many different fields is a formidable task. Explaining why governments do what they do, and trying to learn what the consequences of these many diverse activities are for society, is a serious challenge for political science and the social sciences generally.

Historically public policy has not been the central focus of political science. Instead, political scientists have concerned themselves with the institutions and structures of government, and with political behaviors and processes, rather than the content of public policy itself. "Traditional" political science focused its attention primarily on the institutional structure and the philosophical justification of government. This involved the study of constitutional arrangements, such as federalism, separation of power and judicial review; the powers and duties of official bodies, such as Congress, the President, and courts; inter-governmental relations, the organization and operation of legislative, executive, and judicial agencies; and the philosophies, ideologies, and ethical principles of government. Modern "behavioral" political science focussed its attention primarily on the processes and behaviors associated with government. This involved the study of the sociological and psychological bases of individual and group political behavior; the determinants of voting and other political acts; the functioning of interest groups and political parties; and the description and explanation of various processes and behaviors in the legislative, executive, and judicial arenas. But neither the traditional nor the behavioral political science dealt directly with the *content* of public policy.

Today, political scientists are shifting their attention to public policy—to the description and explanation of the causes and consequences of government activity. Policy analysis is finding out what governments do in education, health, welfare, housing, civil rights, environmental protection, natural resources, defense, and foreign policy; why they do it; and whether it really makes any difference in the lives of their citizens.

Policy analysis involves the systematic identification of the causes and consequences of public policy, the use of scientific standards of inference, and the search for reliability and generality of knowledge.

Perhaps we should note what policy analysis is *not*. It is *not* the advocacy of policy preferences by social scientists, either individually or collectively. However important it may be for social scientists to act in their capacity as (hopefully) enlightened citizens, policy advocacy and policy analysis are separate endeavors. The demand that social science become "relevant" to the problems confronting society is not an invitation to political activism on the part of social scientists. It is rather a call for the systematic application of social science theroy, methodology, and findings to contemporary societal problems. As the distinguished Israeli social scientist, Yehezkel Dror, explains: "There is a big difference between political scientists, even prominent ones, making statements about important policy problems, and the application of political science to policy issues. Application of science requires more than advocacy of predetermind positions with the help of scientific terminology."[1]

The Policy Studies Movement

The new interest in public policy in the social sciences is reflected in many new courses and curricula in public policy studies, new graduate problems and research institutes, new organizations and journals, and a host of articles and books marking the shift in concern in political science from institutions, processes, and behaviors to public policies.

Increasingly the nation's "think tanks" have undertaken

social policy research. Organizations which originally focused on defense problems (notably the Rand Corporation) now devote increasing attention to social problems. This has involved important changes in their methodologies, including the transformation from operations research and systems analysis to broader policy analysis (with much more attention to social and political variables) and to social experimentation. Indeed, in 1970 the Rand Corporation established a Rand graduate institute for policy studies, which set up a three year doctorate program in policy analysis.

A number of new university programs have been established in policy studies. Among these are the Harvard Graduate Program in Public Policy; the Graduate School of Public Affairs at the University of California at Berkeley; the Institute of Public Studies at the University of Michigan; the Lyndon B. Johnson School of Public Affairs at the University of Texas; the Fels Institute of Public Policy Studies at the University of Pennsylvania. And of course in addition to general policy studies programs, specialized institutes, centers, and programs in public health, in environment, urban affairs, law and society, and education, continue policy-relevant research in these fields.

Within the discipline of political science, a new organization has been formed—the Policy Studies Organization which publishes the *Policy Studies Journal*—composed of political scientists and others with an interest in policy research. The journal does not publish the results of policy research, but rather keeps its members informed of developments in policy studies generally and in specific policy fields, notably environmental policy, civil rights policy, economic regulatory policy, electoral policy, foreign policy, crime policy, educational policy, and poverty and welfare policy.

As political scientists become more interested in the causes and consequences of public policies, they will find themselves working alongside of researchers from other disciplines and professions who are equally concerned with public policy. "Policy science" is really a vast domain populated by sociologists, economists, psychologists, educators, public health specialists, social workers, systems analysts, operations research engineers, planners, and others—all of whom have been concerned with the causes and consequences of public policies for decades. Actually, political scientists are latecomers to this domain of policy research. They have a great deal to learn from an impressive body of accumulated knowledge about the methods of design, measurement, and analysis in policy studies. As yet, the division of labor within the policy sciences is unclear. There is a great deal of overlap between the research of political scientists on public policy and the research of other disciplines and professions. But overlapping should not be discouraged; indeed, common scientific endeavors and even occasional replications are far preferable to rigid disciplinary boundaries and resulting myopia which such boundaries encourage.

Public Policy: Assessing Causes and Consequences

Policy analysis can involve the investigation of either the causes or consequences of government policies or programs. In studies of the *causes* of public policy, public policies themselves are the "dependent variables" and analysts seek to explain these policies by reference to "independent variables" —social, economical, technological, or political forces in society which are hypothesized to be determinants of public policy. Let us label such research as "policy determination" research. Policy determination research might focus on such questions as: What is the effect of economic growth on government taxing and spending? What is the effect of public opinion on laws relating to capital punishment, gun control, abortion, and civil rights? Does greater party competition or increased voter participation bring about more liberal policies and welfare, health, or education? What is the impact of racial and religious group activity on the allocation of public monies to schools and colleges? What forces affect the determination of priorities between defense and domestic spending by governments? These are the *kinds* of questions which can be dealt with in "policy determination" research.

In studies of the *consequences* of public policy, public policies themselves become the "independent variables" and the "dependent variables" are the social, economic, or political conditions in society which are hypothesized to be effected by public policy. Let us label such research as "policy impact" research. Examples of the kinds of questions asked in policy impact research are as follows: Will a guaranteed minimum income for all American families reduce or increase joblessness and social dependency? Can black students in ghetto schools receive a quality education through improvements in their neighborhood schools, or must they be bussed out of the ghetto environment for an equal educational opportunity? Who gains and who loses from the present distribution of tax burdens and expenditure benefits, and what will be the impact of tax reform on the redistribution of income in America? Will federal revenue sharing result in any significant alleviation of urban problems—blight, pollution, congestion, crime, or fiscal crisis? These are examples of *kinds* of questions which can be dealt with in policy impact analysis.

Policy Research in Action: The Evaluation of Head Start

But the development of a *policy science* poses many significant problems for the discipline of political science—indeed for the social sciences generally. I would like to turn to two examples of policy relevant research—both dealing with research into the consequences of public policies ("policy impact research"). The purpose of these illustrations will be to explore both the problems and the prospects of a scientific and relevant policy science. The first example is the research undertaken by Westinghouse Learning Corporation and Ohio University on the impact of participation in Head Start programs on the academic success of disadvantaged children. The second example deals with the research undertaken by the University of Wisconsin Institute for Research on Poverty for the U. S. Office of Economic Opportunity into the consequences of various income maintenance schemes on the working behavior of low income families.

When the Economic Opportunity Act of 1964 first authorized the creation of local Community Action Agenices throughout the nation to fight the "war on poverty," the responsibility for devising community anti-poverty projects was placed in the hands of the local participants themselves.[2] But within one year, the office of Economic Opportunity in Washington, and its Director Sargent Shriver, decided that "Head Start" programs were the most desirable anti-poverty projects. OEO "ear-marked" a substantial portion of funds for local Community Action agencies for Head Start programs. The typical local Head Start project was a cooperative program between the Community Action Agency and the local school district. Pre-school children from poor families were given six to eight weeks of special summer preparation before entering kindergarten or first grade. The idea was to give these disadvantaged children a "head start" on formal schooling. But OEO Director Shriver was also aware of the political popularity of the program: the idea of helping prepare disadvantaged children for school elicits more sympathy from the middle class than programs to provide free legal aid for the poor, or helping them get on welfare rolls, or orgaanizing them to fight city hall. Indeed, Head Start turned out to be the most popular program in the "war on poverty." Nearly all of the nation's Community Action agencies operated a Head Start project, and over one-half million children were enrolled throughout the country at the height of the program in the late 1960's. Some communities expanded into full-year Head Start programs, and provided children with health services and improved daily diets. Headstart became OEO's showcase program. As early as 1965 President Johnson declared Head Start to be "battle-tested" and "proven worthy."

The task of evaluating the effectiveness of OEO programs was lodged in OEO itself—in its Office of Research, Plans, Programs and Evaluation (RPP&E). This division proposed a study of the Head Start program in which former Head Start children who were now in the first, second, and third grades of school would be given tests to determine if their "intellectual and social-personal development" was any different from that of disadvantaged children who had never attended Head Start. The scores of the Head Start group would be compared with the non-Head Start (control) group. But Head Start officials *within* OEO were discomforted by the thought of a formal evaluation of their program. They argued that educational success was not the only goal of the program—that child health and nutrition, and even parental involvement in a community program, were equally important goals. They also opposed the *ex post facto* research design, arguing instead for before and after testing of Head Start children. After much internal debate, Director Shriver ordered an evaluative study, and in 1968 a contract was given to Westinghouse Learning Corporation and Ohio University to perform the research.

When Richard Nixon assumed the Presidency in January 1969, hints of negative findings had already filtered up to the

White House. In his first comments on the poverty program, Nixon alluded to studies showing the long term effect of Head Start as "extremely weak." This teaser prompted the press and Congress to call for the release of the Westinghouse Report. OEO claimed that the results were still "too preliminary" to be revealed. However, after a Congressional committee investigation and considerable political pressure, OEO finally released the report in June, 1969.[3]

The Report stated that the researchers had randomly selected 104 Head Start projects across the country. Seventy percent were summer projects and thirty percent were full-year projects. Children who had gone on from these programs to the first, second, and third grades in local schools were matched in socioeconomic background with children in the same grades who had *not* attended Head Start. All children were given a series of tests covering various aspects of cognitive and affective development (the Metropolitan Readiness Test, the Illinois Test of Psycholinguistic Abilities, the Stanford Achievement Test, the Childrens Self-Concept Test, etc.) The parents of both groups of children were interviewed, and teachers were asked to rate both groups of children on achievement and motivation.

The unhappy results can be summarized as follows:

1. Summer programs were ineffective in producing any gains in cognitive and affective development that persist into the early elementary grades.

2. Full-year programs produced only marginally effective gains for certain sub-groups, mainly black children in central cities.

3. However, parents of Head Start enrollees voiced strong approval of the program.

Head Start officials reacted predictably in condemning the Report. Liberals attacked the Report because they believed that President Nixon would use it to justify major cutbacks

in OEO. The *New York Times* reported the findings under
the headline "Head Start Report Held 'Full of Holes'." The
New York Times warned liberals "that Congress or the Administration will seize upon the report's generally negative
conclusions as an excuse to downgrade or discard the Head
Start Program" (not an unreasonable action in the light of
the findings, but politically unacceptable to the liberal community).[4] Academicians moved to the defense of the war on
poverty by attacking various methodological aspects of the
study.[5] In short, scientific assessment of the impact of Head
Start was drowned in a sea of political controversy. Despite
Head Start's proven ineffectiveness in improving the abilities
of children, it remains a politically popular program. Even
President Nixon was obliged to "save" the Head Start Program when he initiated measures to phase out the Community Action Program and OEO itself. In 1974, Head Start
was transferred from OEO to the Department of Health
Education and Welfare.

*Policy Research In Action: The Guaranteed Income
Experiments*

Our second example of policy-relevant research—the New
Jersey Guaranteed Income Experiments—is a rare example
of government-sponsored "policy experimentation": the systematic selection of experimental and control groups, the
application of the policy under study to the experimental
group only, and a careful comparison of differences between
the experimental and the control group after the application
of the policy.

The experiment was designed to resolve some serious questions about the impact of welfare payments on the incentives
for poor people to work.

Debates over welfare reform had generated certain questions which social science presumably could answer with careful, controlled experimentation. Would a guaranteed family income reduce the incentive to work? If payments are made to poor families with employable male heads, will the men drop out of the labor force? Would the level of the income guarantee, or the steepness of the reductions of payments with increases in earning, make any difference in working behavior? Since current welfare programs do not provide a guaranteed minimum family income, or make payments to families with employable males, or graduate payments in relation to earnings, these questions could only be answered through *policy experimentation.*

To assess the impact of guaranteed incomes on families with able-bodied men, the Office of Economic Opportunity sponsored a three-year social experiment involving 1,350 families in New Jersey and Pennsylvania.[6] The research was undertaken by the University of Wisconsin's Institute of Research on Poverty under the direction of economist Harold Watts. To ascertain the effects of different levels of guaranteed income, four guarantee levels were established. Some families were chosen to receive 50 percent of the Social Security Administration's poverty line income, others 75 percent, others 100 percent, and still others 125 percent. In order to ascertain the effects of graduated payments in relation to earnings, some families had their payments reduced by 30 percent of their outside earnings, other 50 percent, and still others 70 percent. Finally, a control sample was observed —families who received no payments at all in the experiment, but were matched in every way with families who were receiving payments.

The experiment was begun in 1968 and planned to run for three years. But political events moved swiftly and soon engulfed the study. In 1969 President Nixon proposed the Family Assistance Plan (FAP) to Congress which initially at least guaranteed all families a minimum income of 50 percent of the poverty line and a payment reduction of 50 percent of outside earnings. The Nixon Administration had not waited to learn the results of the OEO experiment before introducing FAP. Prsident Nixon wanted welfare reform to be his priority domestic legislation and the bill was symbolically number HR 1 (House of Representatives Bill No. 1).

After the FAP bill had been introduced, the Nixon Administration pressured OEO to produce favorable supporting evidence on behalf of the guaranteed income—specifically, evidence that a guaranteed income at the levels and graduated sublevels proposed in FAP would *not* reduce incentives to work among the poor. The OEO obliged by hastily publishing a short report, "Preliminary Results of the New Jersey Graduated Work Incentive Experiment,"[7] which purported to show that there were no differences in the outside earnings of families receiving guaranteed incomes (experimental group) and those who were not (control group).

The director of the research, economics professor Harold Watts of the University of Wisconsin, warned "the evidence from this preliminary and crude analysis of the earliest results is less than ideal." But he concluded that: "No evidence has ben found in the urban experiment to support the belief that negative-tax-type income maintenance programs will produce large disincentives to work and consequent reductions in earnings." Moreover, the early results indicated that families in all of the separate experimental groups, with different guaranteed minimums and different graduated payment schedules, behaved in a fashion similar to each other and to the control group receiving no payments at all. Predictably, later results published a few months ago confirmed the preliminary results which were produced to assist the FAP bill in Congress.

The whole excursion into government-sponsored policy impact experimentation, however, raises a series of important questions. First of all, are government-sponsored research projects predisposed to produce results supportive of popular reform proposals? Are social scientists, whose personal political values are generally liberal and reformist, inclined to produce findings in support of liberal reform measures? Would the OEO have rushed to produce "preliminary findings" in the New Jersey experiment *if* these had shown that the guarantees did in fact reduce the incentive to work? Or would such early results be set aside as "too preliminary" to publish? Since the participants in the experiment know that they were singled out for experimentation, did they behave differently than they would if the program had been applied universally? Would the work ethic be impaired if *all* American families were guaranteed a minimum income for life, rather than a few selected families for a temporary period of time? Thus, the questions raised by this experiment affect not only the issues of welfare policy, but also the validity of policy research itself.

Policy Analysis and Policy-Making:
Knowledge into Action

What should be the appropriate role of the social scientist in the policy-making process? All scientific disciplines face the continuing problem of making their knowledge useful to society. Specifically, the policy sciences face the question of determining what should be their appropriate relationship with government. On this question there is no real consensus among social scientists who study public policy.

Some social scientists argue for minimizing direct disciplinary links with government out of their concern about the development of scientific theory. Direct ties with government frequently mandate applied social science research aimed to providing solutions to immediate, narrowly defined problems or remedying specific programmatic ventures. These exercises in "applied research" seldom produce general scientific knowledge—at least not in proportion to the energies, resources, and money spent on them. Social science should not divert its limited resources from "basic research" in the developing and testing of scientific theory.*

Many policy analysts argue that it is better to provide the policy-maker with whatever little knowledge is produced by social science, than have policy-makers act in the absence of any knowledge at all. Presumably, if we know something about the forces shaping public policy and the consequences of specific policies, then we are in a better position to know how individuals, groups, or governments can act to achieve their goals. Even if social scientists cannot accurately predict the impact of *future* policies, they can at least attempt to measure the impact of *current* and *past* public policies and to make this knowledge available to policy-makers. But we do not need to rely exclusively on "rules of thumb" or "muddling through" or "it sounds like a good idea" or the rhetoric of interested parties in approaching policy questions.

The fact is, of course, that a number of social scientists do advise policy-makers. They serve as advisors to presidents, as

---

* A dffierent kind of argument for minimizing ties between social scientists and policy-makers is often advanced by radical critics of the American political system. Some social scientists do not want to have any connection with government—arguing that American society and the political system is morally corrupt and that social scientists who let themselves be co-opted to work within the system can only be corrupted by it. They argue that social science can only gain a "radical" perspective by functioning outside of the system, criticizing it, and pressing for radical change.

members of governmental commissions; they work as staffs of commissions and congressional committees; they serve as consultants to governmental agencies; they testify before legislative committees; and so on. The real question is whether the policy-making process or social sciences themselves should be restructured in any way to facilitate and encourage communication between scholars and policy-makers, and if so, how?

The "knowledge into action" problem is a serious one. There are many obstacles to effective communication between social scientists and policy-makers. Let me describe a few of these problems.

The policy-maker is searching for guides for effective governmental action. He is "decision-oriented" in his approach. In contrast, the policy scientists usually seeks to test and develop theories about the causes and consequences of public policy. His approach is "theory-oriented." These contrasting approaches underlie the "knowledge into action" problem —the effective utilization of social science research in the formulation of public policy. Let us explore some of the implications of the contrasting approaches of the scholar and policy-maker for effective communication between the policy analyst and the policy-maker.

1. *Problem-Oriented Versus Theory-Directed Research.* The policy-maker confronts a societal problem which is real rather than theoretical. Its solution may, or may not, contribute to the development of general scientific theories about public policy. In contrast, the scholar originates his research as a test to some general theoretical proposition about the causes or consequences of public policy. His object is to develop a general scientific theory which is reliable and which applies to different government agencies in different areas. For the policy analyst, the ultimate product is the contri-

bution to existing scientific knowledge"; to the policy-maker
the value of policy analysis is the public policy modified by
an understanding of its consequences. Of course everyone
knows that good problem solving contributes to scientific theory development, and that research which is well formulated
from the theoretical standpoint can have important practical
problem solving implication. But it is difficult to whisk away
altogether the problem of priorities in problem-oriented versus theory-directed research. Too often the policy scientists
present the policy-maker with a scientific research report
which he is unable to utilize in folicy formation.

2. *Time-Limited Versus Cumulative Research.* In research
on public policy, the policy-maker knows that a decision
will be made at a certain time, that action will be taken at
that time, and it cannot be based on information that is only
available later. In contrast, the scholar realizes that scientific
knowledge advances at a pace determined by theoretical
development and research results. The policy-maker places
greater value on partial information available at the
time of action than he does complete scientific knowledge
acquired after the time for action has passed. The implication
of these differences is not trivial. For policy anaylists to provide policy-makers with effective guides to action, they must
be prepared to provide partial results at various time points—
design their research to facilitate a steady cumulation of research results that can aid policy decisions, rather than a
single complete research result at the end of their work.

3. *Probable Approximation Versus Methodological Elegance.* Another contrast closely related to the timing problem
is that the policy-maker prefers research which provides a
high probability of giving approximately the right guides to
public action, while the scholar seeks scientific rigor and
methodological elegance. In other words, the policy-maker
seeks predictions which are good approximations of what

will happen in the real world. The scholar is concerned with the real world too, but he drives his predictions from scientific theory. His sophisticated predictive techniques may give excellent results if they are correct, but they may be far off if some of the assumptions of his theories are not met. Frequently, simple projections of past trends are better predictions of real world conditions in the future than scientifically derived, methodologically elegant predictions. The policy-maker values predictions which are approximately right, rather than predictions which are derived from and correspond to scientific theory.

4. *Explantion Versus Intervention.* The scholar is concerned with explaining the causes and consequences of public policy, and he gives the greatest attenion to those conditions which explain the largest proportion of variance of public policy or its consequences. In contrast, the policy-maker is interested in intervention: he gives greatest attention to those variables which are subject to governmental manipulation. Scientific research which reveals the overwhelming impact of underlying economic and social conditions on poverty, or education, or ill-health, or any other other social problem, can only frustrate policy-makers if it gives them no immediate policy handles for remedial action. (If human behavior turned out to be 90% a function of height, there is really no point in telling the policy-maker this because people can't be stretched. The policy-maker is more interested in the 10% of the behavior which may be manipulated rather than the 90% which is predetermined.) The policy-maker seeks to pose questions which involve policy variables and their consequences; the scholar seeks to explain societal conditions which may or may not be affected by public policy. When policy analysts explain societal problems but do not distinguish between causes which can be affected by public policy and those which cannot, they fail to give the policy-

maker anything that he can use because they give him no handles for action.

5. *Competitive Versus Self-Corrective Research.* The policy-maker's different time perspective does not allow the full self-correcting processes that exist in scientific research. For the policy-maker, wrong answers can be costly if not disastrous. In contrast, in scientific research, one researcher's results are subject to the prolonged scrutiny of his scientific colleagues who find it in their professional interest to show him wrong. For example, scientific researchers attempt to carry out replications of research of other researchers; they gain the attention of the disipline if they show that the results are not replicable. This constitutes a built-in adversary or competitive structure which is the primary self-correcting device for science. But the policy-maker does not have time for a prolonged process of self-correction. Policy analysts can be biased and incompetent. The plethora of contradictory recommendations emanating for the social sciences about nearly every problem under consideration should warn policy-makers about trusting blindly in the results of social science research. Perhaps the policy-maker's only solution is to commission multiple research groups under the auspices of differently interested researchers, to study the same problems. In other words, the policy-maker might be well-advised to substitute a simultaneous competitive research structure for the prolonged self-corrective processes of science.

6. *Precision Versus Communication.* The development of scientific theory requires exceptional clarity and preciseness of terminology; the result is frequently considered "jargon" by the policy-maker. The policy-maker is a user, a consumer, of research, and while he is knowledgeable about public pollicy and social conditions, he is not likely to be himself a so-

cial scientist. Effective communication between the policy analyst and the policy-maker involves two sets of translations: translation from the problem of the world of reality and policy into the world of scientific theory and method, and then the translation of the research results back into the world of reality and policy. If the policy analyst does not understand the requirements of effective policy formation, or if the policy-maker cannot understand the practical implications of scientific research results, there will continue to be a gap between research and policy formation, regardless of the relevance or quality of the research itself. Ordinarily a scholar does not address himself to these translation problems, because scientific research operates within the realm of disciplinary, scholarly discourse. But the translation task cannot be left solely to the policy-maker himself. If policy research is to be used in policy formation, techniques and habits must be developed by social scientists to cope with the problems of translation.

The Symbolic Use of Policy

Another aspect of public policy which frequently generates different perspectives for the policy analyst and the policy-maker centers about the symbolic functions of public policy. Frequently, the sensitive policy-maker is more aware than the scientist of the symbolic impact of policy. By the symbolic impact we refer to the perceptions that individuals have of government action and their attitudes toward it. Even if government policies do not succeed in reducing dependency, or eliminating poverty, or preventing crime, and so on, this may be a rather minor objection to them if the failure of government to *try* to do these things would lead to the view that society is "not worth saving." Individuals, groups, and whole societies frequently judge public policy in terms

of its good intentions rather than its tangible accomplish-
ments. Sociologist Edward Suchman distinguishes between
policy "evaluation" and "evaluative research."⁸ Evaluation
refers to the general popularity and public appraisal of a
program. Evaluative research refers to systematic analysis
of the real impact of a program in terms of desired results.
The implication is that very popular programs may have little
positive impact, and vice versa.

The policies of government may tell us more about the
aspirations of a society and its leadership than about actual
conditions. Policies do more than affect change in societal
conditions; they also help hold men together and maintain an
orderly state. For example, a government "war on poverty"
may not have any significant impact on the poor, but it reassures moral men, the affluent as well as the poor, that government "cares" about poverty. Whatever the failures of the
anti-poverty program in tangible respects, its symbolic value
may be more than redeeming. For example, whether the fair
housing provisions of the Civil Rights Act of 1968 can be en-
forced or not, the fact that it is national policy to forbid dis-
crimination in the sale or rental of housing reassures men of
all races that their government does not condone such acts.
There are many more examples of public policy serving as a
symbol of what society aspires to be.

The subjective condition of the nation is clearly as important as the objective condition. Once upon a time "politics"
was described as "who gets what, when, and how." The
smoke-filled room where patronage and pork were dispensed
has been replaced with the talk-filled room, where rhetoric
and image are dispensed. What governments *say* is as important as what governments *do*. Television has made the
image of public policy as important as the policy itself. Systematic policy analysis concentrates on what governments
do, why they do it, and what difference it makes. It devotes

less attention to what governments *say*. Perhaps this is a weakness in policy analysis. The focus of the policy analyst is primarily upon activities of governments, rather than the rhetoric of governments.

2 POLICY ANALYSIS: STATES AND NATIONS

The Myopia of Political Science

Certainly the recent progress in policy studies in political science has been encouraging. Yet there are serious obstacles to the development of a systematic policy science within the discipline of political science. Let me describe two of these obstacles—which I have labeled "the professional and ideological myopia of political science."

1. *The profesional myopia of political science* is the narrow and restricted definition of the boundaries of the discipline—a definition which limits the attention of political scientists to governmental institutions and political proecsses. The professional preoccupation of political scientists has been with the characteristics of political systems. The result is a professional predisposition to assert the importance of political system characteristics in determining the causes and consequences of public policy. For example, political scientists may explain public policy in terms of successful interest group lobbying, or Presidential influence in Congress, or the strength or weakness of governors in dealing with state legislators, or the cohesion of the Democratic or Republican par-

ties in Congress, or the extent of malapportionment in the states, or the effects of the seniority system in Congressional committee activity, or the constitutional arrangements limiting or augmenting the power of Congress, Courts, or the President. But if political science is to become a *policy science*, poltical scientists must be prepared to search for the determinants of public policy among economic, social, cultural, historical, and technological factors, as well as political system characteristics. Political scientists must also be prepared to examine the consequences of public policies in areas as diverse as education, welfare, health, housing, the environment, national defense, the economy, and foreign affairs. Clearly, then, for political science to become a policy science, it must discard narrow definitions of what is "political" and examine the full range of forces shaping public policy.

2. *The ideological myopia of political science* is the prevailing commitment of the discipline to democratic "pluralism." The pluralist ideology which pervades our discipline directs the attention of the political scientist to political participation, electoral processes and behaviors, interest group activity, and party competition, *because these processes are highly valued in pluralist political theory*. The result is an ideological predisposition of political scientists to assert the importance of participation and competition in determining the causes and consequences of public policies. Yet, despite the importance of participation, competition, and equality as *political values*, we must not make the mistake of assuming that they are influential *determinants of public policy*. Moreover, there is an ideological predisposition among political scientists to believe that democratic-pluralist political systems produce "better" public policies than non-pluralistic systems —quality educational programs, liberal welfare benefits, comprehensive health care, progressive tax schemes, etc.

These professional and ideological predispositions operate

to reinforce each other. Political scientists are predisposed to believe 1) that political system characteristics are important determinants of the causes and consequences of public policies; and 2) that competition, paticipation, and equality in representation produce "good" public policies. Either of these propositions *may* be correct. It is not my intention to dispute them. My point is that a systematic policy science must treat these propositions as *hypotheses* to be tested, not as prior assumptions. My plea is for a scientific posture in politicial science which designs policy research in such a way so as to control, in so far as possible, our predispositions and values.

Some Discomforting Findings: States and Nations

Policy analysis is still in its infancy. Our findings regarding the causes and consequences of government activity are still very tentative and our theories and models are still very underdeveloped. However, some initial studies of the determinants of public policy raise serious doubts about the traditional assumptions of political scientists—assumptions regarding 1) the importance of political system characteristics as determinants of public policy, and 2) the influence of democratic pluralist political structures on the content of public policy.

The purpose of this essay is to survey some policy research studies involving *states and nations*—studies which raise doubts about these traditional assumptions. The really remarkable fact is that different scholars working with different types of political systems—states and nations—have all produced roughly similar findings regarding the influence of political system characteristics on the content of public policy.

Let us turn first to research on public policy in the American states, where many of the key issues were first raised.

Then we will briefly examine some thought-provoking research on the determinants of public policy among *nations*. The exciting prospect in policy research is that someday all of this research will come together; that scholars will begin to test proposition about the behavior of *political systems*—cities, states, and nations; and that truly general theories of government activity can be developed.

Policy Analysis: The American States

Within the discipline of political science, significant advances in policy analysis have occurred in the field of state government. Traditionally this field was not renowned for systematic research; instead, it reflected traditional concerns for governmental institutions and administrative arrangements, party competition and voter participation, and structural reforms. But fifty separate state political systems offered scientifically-minded political scientists an excellent opportunity to employ non-experimental comparative research designs in their studies of the linkages between environmental conditions, political systems, and public policies. Fortunately, if only for the sake of analysis, there are marked differences among the American states in economic dvelopment levels, in many political system characteristics, and in a significant range of policies.

The traditional literature in American state politics instructed students that characteristics of state political systems —particularly two party competition, voter participation, and apportionment—had a direct bearing on public policy. Since political scientists devoted most of their time to studying what happened *within* the political system, it was natural for them to believe that the political processes which they studied were important determinants of public policy. Moreover, the belief that competition, participation, and equality in representation had important consequences for public policy also squared with the value placed upon these variables in the prevailing pluralist ideology. States with higher voter participation, intense party competition, and fair apportionment—usually northern and midwestern states—suggested a normative model of pluralist democracy, which was expected to produce "good" public policies—liberal welfare benefits, generous educational spending, progressive taxation, advanced health and hospital care, and so on. In contrast, states with low voter participation, and absence of party competition, and unfair apportionment—usually southern states—suggested a type of political system which was widely deplored among American political scientists. Moreover, such political systems were believed to produce meager welfare benefits, miserly educational spending, regressive taxation, archaic health and hospital programs, and so on. (It is intellectually fashionable now to regard these beliefs as mere strawmen erected by economic determinists to attack. But at the time these beliefs were central assertions in the state politics literature; assertions which had long nurtured on the apriori reasoning and case studies of V. O. Key, Jr., Dwane Lockard, John Fenton, and others.[2])

Economic research had suggested very early that the public policies of state and local governments were closely related to their economic resources. Although this economic literature was largely overlooked by political scientists, economists contributed a great deal to the systematic analysis of state and local public policies. Systematic analysis of the economic determinants of state and local government expenditures began with the publication of Solomon Fabricant's *The Trend of Government Activity in the United States Since 1900.*[3] Fabricant found that per capita income, population density, and urbanization explained more than 72 percent of the variation among the states in total spending. Of these three economic variables, he found that *per capita income* showed the strongest relationship to expenditures. Another economist, Glenn F. Fisher, continued Fabricant's analysis of the economic determinants of state and local spending into the 1960s.[4] Fisher added additional economic variables (e.g., percentage of families with less than $2,000 annual income, percentage increase in population, percentage of adults with less than five years schooling) and was able to explain even more of the interstate differences in state and local spending. Again, like Fabricant, Fisher found that per capita income was the strongest single factor associated with state and local expenditures. Later, economists Sachs and Harris added to this research literature by considering the effect of federal grants-in-aid on state and local government expenditure.[5] They observed that federal grants tended to free the states from the constraints of their own economic resources. Federal grants were "outside money" to state and local government officials which permitted them to fund programs at levels beyond their own resources. Hence, they noted the decline in the closeness of the relationship to economic resources in state and local spending, particularly in the fields with the heaviest federal involvement: welfare and health.

The traditional state politics literature overlooked this economic research into the determinants of public policy. Nonetheless, some early research in state politics suggested that party competition and voter participation were themselves heavily impacted by economic variables. A number of scholars—Ranney and Kendall, Key, Schlesinger, and Golembiewski, for example[6]—indicated that economic factors affected the level of interparty competition; they reported statistically significant associations between urbanism, income, industrialization, and classifications of party competition among the states. Knowledge of this linkage between economic forces and the political system *should* have suggested to political scientists that they test to see if competition and participation *independently* affected public policies, or whether both competition and participation and public policies were all determined by economic factors. For example, if it was shown that, in general, wealthy states have more party competition than poor states, then it might turn out that differences in levels of educational spending between competitive and noncompetitive states are really a product of the fact that the former are wealthy and the latter are poor. In other words, policy differences between the states might be attributable to wealth rather than to party competition.

The first hint that pluralist political variables—party competition, voter participation, Democratic and Republican control of state government, and malapportionment—might *not* be as influential in determining levels of public taxing, spending, benefits, and service, as commonly supposed, came in an important research effort by Richard E. Dawson and James A. Robinson in 1963. These political scientists examined the linkages between socioeconomic variables (income, urbanization, industrialization), the level of interparty competition, and nine public welfare policies. They concluded that:

> High levels of inter-party competition are highly interrelated both to socioeconomic factors and to social welfare legislation, but the degree of inter-party competition does not seem to possess the important intervening influence between socioeconomic factors and liberal welfare programs that our original hypothesis and theoretical schemes suggested.[7]

In 1966, I published a comprehensive analysis of public policy in the American states, *Politics, Economics, and the Public*.[8] I described the linkage between four economic development variables (urbanization, industralization, wealth, and education), four political system characteristics (Democratic or Republican control of state government, the degree of interparty competition, the level of voter turn out, and the extent of malapportionment), and over ninety separate policy output measures in education, health, welfare, highways, corrections, taxations, and public regulation. This research produced some findings that were very unsettling for political scientists. These four commonly described characteristics of pluralist political systems were found to have *less* effect on public policy in the states *than* environmental variables reflecting the level of economic development. Most of the associations which occur between these pluralist variables and policy measures are really a product of the fact that economic development influences *both* political system characteristics and policy outcomes. Of course, I noted several policy areas where political factors remained important, and I identified certain policy areas where federal programs tended to offset the impact of economic resources on state policies. Yet in the attempt to generalize about the determinants of public policy in the states, I concluded that *on the whole* economic resources were more influential in shaping state policies than any of the political variables previously thought to be important in policy determination. Doubtlessly these findings disturbed scholars who felt more comfortable with the reassuring notion of pluralist democracy that "politics counts."

But the findings themselves—regarded almost as commonplace by economists—were really not so important as the impetus this study gave to the policy analysis movement. A number of scholars were stimulated to reexamine systematically the traditional wisdom of the state politics field. The result was an outpouring of systematic social science research which employed rigorous and comparative methods to test propositions about the determinants of public policies, particularly at the state and local levels.[9] New and more sophis-

ticated methodological techniques were introduced;[10] some
primitive causal modeling was begun;[11] additional political
variables were tested for their policy impact;[12] some policy
outputs other than levels of public expenditures and services
were examined;[13] changes over time were described and an-
alyzed;[14] some research findings were modified and exceptions to general propositions were described;[15] some more
discerning theoretical notions about public policy were developed;[16] and "non-additive models" (where the *logs* of variable values are used in regression problems) were shown to
explain slightly larger proportional variance than ordinary
linear regression models.[17] In short the whole subfield of the
discipline of political science grew to maturity in a very short
period of time.[18]

State Policy Studies: The Professional Response

Implicit in much of this literature, however, is a noticeable
reluctance to accept the view that political system characteristics, particularly those reflecting pluralist values of competition and participation, may possess less policy-relevance
than economic resources. Indeed, there appears to be a great
deal of scrambling about by scholars ideologically committed
to proving that party competition, voter participation, partisanship, and apportionment do indeed influence public
policy. A representative sample of the near-panic among
some political scientists produced by findings about economic determinants can be found in *Polity:*

> It is our contention in this paper that the explanation
> for these findings lies in the choice, or inadvertent adoption,
> of a particular model of the policy process which is neither
> accurate, reliable, precise, nor appropriate. . . . Our response
> to the problem is to propose a model of the policy-making
> process which will eliminate many of difficulties to which
> the *unacceptable* findings are attributable. By attacking

the underlying theoretical notions, by making the theoretical relationships clear and more meaningful, and by specifying the variables and variable relationships more completely, we hope to be able to put the question of the determinants of public policy in its *proper* theoretical perspective —a perspective that may well generate a set of findings that will be more *compatible with our traditional understanding* of the operation of politics and government in the formation of public policy.[19] [Italics Added]

Of course, governmental institutions, administrative arrangements, and political processes may indeed help to determine the content of public policy. This is a question which we must try to answer in our research. But we should not insist that political variables influence policy outcomes simply because our traditional training and wisdom in political science has told us that political variables are important.

Nonetheless, there have been some interesting challenges to the general direction of the findings regarding the influence of economic resources on public policy. Richard Hofferbert studied the relationship between economic resources, political variables, and public policy in the American states from 1890 to 1960.[20] He detected a slight *decline* in the strengths of relationships between economic resources and policy outcomes over this time period. He reasoned that a generally high level of economic development provides political decision-makers with greater latitude in policy choices and tends to free them from the restraints imposed by limited resources. While economic resources continue to be the major determinant of public policy, the implication of Hofferbert's study is that in the future the *attitudes of political leaders* may be increasingly important in determining levels of public spending and service.

Other researchers focused their attention on a narrower range of policies which are independently associated with

competition and participation. Two widely acclaimed studies—a regression exercise by Cnudde and McCrone and a
factor analytic exercise by Sharkansky and Hofferbert[21]—indicate that party competition may indeed have some independent influence in the determination of welfare benefits. In
these studies, V. O. Key's traditional notion of the liberali-
zing effects of competition is narrowed to a single set of policy measures—welfare benefits. According to Cnudde and
McCrone: "Party competition, then, may not have an appre-
ciable impact on some types of policies, but Key's discussion
would lead us to specify the conditions under which it would
have its greatest effect: the have-not oriented policies." There
is nothing wrong with this, of course. But these findings do
not really "contrast" with earlier efforts to generalize about
the relative influence of economic resources in determining a
broad array of policy variables in education, welfare, health,
highways, corrections, taxing, and spending. However ideologically satisfying the results of these studies must have been
for democratic pluralists, they do not justify the "conclusion"
that "the (economic) model now predominant in state politics literature rests on shakey empirical foundations."

What is required in studying the policy impact of political
competition and participation is more empirical testing and
less ideological disputation. Perhaps the best example of the
type of research which can produce a better understanding
of the complex forces shaping state policy is a study of welfare aid for dependent children in the fifty states by political
scientist Gary L. Tompkins.[22] He carefully constructed a sequential model in which industrialization, income, and ethnicity were hypothesized as factors affecting competition and
participation, and all of these variables were hypothesized
in turn as factors affecting aid to dependent children. He
then subjected his model to path analytic testing (See Chapter 4). The results suggested 1) that income affects welfare

aid *through* its effect on interparty competition, 2) that interparty competition does have *some* direct influence on increasing welfare aid, 3) that voter turnout has *no* direct or indirect effect on welfare aid, 4) and that *ethnicity* has the strongest link to welfare aid. The strong positive effect of ethnicity on welfare spending per dependent child was surprising, and it should warn us that our explanations to date are still very tentative.

Thus, a promising avenue of research may be to search for political system characteristics *other than* competition, participation, partisanship, and apportionment, which may be more influential than these pluralist variables in the determination of public policy. Of course this may involve the abandonment of a great deal of traditional literature in the field, but the effort may prove worthwhile. For example, it may turn out that measures of *professionalism* or *reformism* in political systems are independently associated with a wide range of public policies. Reformism has been an important political movement in American state and local government for over a century. The reform style of politics emphasizes, among other things, the replacement of political patronage practices with a professional civil service system; the professionalism of government services; the reorganization of government to promote efficiency and accountability; and a preference for a non-partisan atmosphere in government. At the municipal level, reformism has promoted the manager form of government, nonpartisan election, home rule, at-large constituencies, and comprehensive planning. At the state level, reformism has emphasized a professional state administration, a reduction in the number of separately elected executive officials, civil service coverage of state employees, and a well-paid, well-staffed, professional state legislature. There is some evidence that reformism and professionalism are more influential than pluralism in the determination

of a number of important state policies.[23] Further research
on the impact of professionalism and reformism in government is certainly indicated.

Another promising avenue of research effort is the search
for policy variables other than levels of public taxing,
spending benefits, and services. Certainly there are many
dimensions to the general concept—public policy. It is frequently asserted, albeit seldom demonstrated, that there
are important qualitative or distributional aspects of public
policy which are determined by political factors, rather than
economic resources. For example, Fry and Winters under-
took to measure the progressivity and regressivity of both
taxing and spending in the American states.[24] Certainly the
distribution of burdens and benefits among income groups
of government taxing and spending is an important qualitative aspect of public policy—one that is not reflected in
measures of the level of government taxing, spending, benefits, and services. Fry and Winters find that voter participation, civil service coverage, and legislative professionalism
have a significant independent effect in bringing about progressivity in the distribution of taxing and spending burdens.
They contend (erroneously) that they have "reversed" the
findings of earlier research; but , of course, what they have
really done is show that political variables affect the *distribution* of taxing and spending burdens. They have not challenged the original findings about *levels* of public taxing,
spending, benefits, and service. However, a recent re-analy-
sis of Fry and Winters' data cast some doubt on their claim
that political variables had a significant independent affect
on their disributional measure, or even an effect greater than
a state's economic resources. John L. Sullivan contends that
Fry and Winters erred in their analysis and that is it "unclear"
whether political variables have any affect on the distribution
of tax and spending burdens which is independent of

wealth.[25] Nontheless, Fry and Winters' effort deserves praise.

Less praiseworthy, perhaps, has been the assertion that because economic variables fail to explain *all* of the variation in public policy, or even half of the variation in a number of specific policy measures, that this fact is itself evidence of the influence of political factors. Unfortunately, my colleague, Ira Sharkansky on several occasions has called attenion to *un*explained variation in levels of government taxing, spending, benefits, and services in the states.[26] (*Un*explained variation is one minus explained variation; for example, if economic resources explain 63 percent of the variation among the states and per pupil expenditures, the remaining 37 percent is unexplained by economic resources.) Now certainly there is room for continued research on additional determinants of public policy. But social science rarely produces complete explanations of anything. Unexplained variation may be a product of poor measurement or a product of the combined effect of thousands of other factors at work in the states. The implication by Professor Sharkansky and others that unexplained variation is evidence of the influence of politics, tells us more about the professional and ideological predispositions of political scientists than anything else.

The Federal Influence in State Policy-Making

Federal grant-in-aid money is now a very important resource of state and local government. Federal grants now account for one-third of all state government revenues and one-sixth of all local government revenues. This "outside money" tends to free states from some of the constraints of their own limited economic resources on levels of public spending and services in the state. Thus, in explaining state policies, we must consider federal grant-in-aid money as an important economic resource and influential independent variable.

Economists have long been aware of the importance of federal aid as a determinant of state and local spending policies. Economists Seymour Sachs and Robert Harris noticed that in 1960 environmental resources were losing some of their explanatory power in relation to state and local spending, particularly in the areas of welfare and health.[27] Specifically, Sachs and Harris noted that the ability of income, population density, and urbanization to explain variation in total state and local spending had declined from 72 percent in 1942 to 53 percent in 1960. They particularly noted the decline in the explanatory power of these three variables in the welfare (from 45 percent in 1942 to 11 percent in 1960) and health (from 72 percent in 1942 to 44 percent in 1960). They suggested that the decline in the explanatory power of economic resources could be attributed to the intervening effect of federal grants-in-aid, particularly in the welfare and health fields. They reasoned that federal grants were freeing the states from the constraints of their own economic resources. Federal grants were viewed as "outside money" by state and local government officials which permitted them to fund programs at levels beyond their own resources. Hence the decline of the closeness of their relationship between economic resources and state and local spending, particularly in the fields with the heaviest involvement: welfare and health. I replicated the Sachs and Harris study for 1970 and confirmed the Sachs and Harris findings.[28] When per capita federal grants-in-aid are included as independent variables, together with environmental varia- bles—income, education, and urbanization—the proportion of explained variance increases noticeably in the health and welfare fields. For example, in the welfare field, the pro- portion of the explained variance leaps from 17 percent (using only environmental variables) to 48 percent (with the inclusion of federal aid). This means that a state's economic resources have relatively little to do with its *welfare* spending; federal policy is a primary determinant of state and local spending in this field. It should be noted, however, that income remains the single most important determinant of state and local spending for all other functions. Sachs and Harris themselves concluded: "per capita income remains the most important determinant of expenditures even after the federal aid variables are added."

Economists also reported that *change* in state and local government expenditures was more closely related to changes in per capita federal grants than to changes in any other independent variable.[29] In short, there is evidence that changes in federal policy resulting in different patterns of federal grant-in-aid monies to the states has the most direct and immediate effect on changes in state policies.

Thus, no one denies the importance of federal grants-in-aid in shaping the state policy. However, there is some confusion about how federal aid should be conceptualized. Economists generally consider federal aid as an economic resource which together with the state's own resources can be utilized by state policy-makers in the determination of levels of public spending and services. My own treatment of federal grants as "outside money" is similar to the conceptualization employed by most economists. The fact that this "outside money" reduced somewhat the closeness of the relationship between state policies and state economic resources does *not* contradict the general notion that economic constraints are the most important forces shaping public policy. On the contrary, these findings confirm that notion by suggesting that federal money acts to free states from some of the constraints of their own limited economic resources. And indeed "equalization" of resources is a familiar theme of the rhetoric surrounding many federal aid programs.

However, some scholars have conceptualized federal aid

as a "political variable" which "pre-empts" the effect of economic resources on state policy. Simply labeling federal aid
as a "political variable" rather than an "economic resource"
enables one to "demonstrate" the increasing importance of a
"political variable" in explaining state policy in recent
years.[30] But the importance of economic resources, whether
derived from within the state or from the federal government,
in shaping state policy cannot be altered by conceptual re-
labeling of packages. Indeed the attempt to relabel federal
aid a "political variable" is further evidence of the professional and ideological blinders of political scientists. Apparently it makes some political scientists feel better to label
federal grants-in-aid as a "political variable" and thereby
reassert, albeit disingenuously, the policy relevance of their
own discipline.

An even more self-defeating theoretical posture was taken
by Douglas D. Rose, who argued that virtually all studies of
policy differences among the states are wrongheaded.[31] Rose
atacked all state policy research on the grounds that 1) variance among the states is less than the variance among individuals, and that as a consequence, studies of state politics
are "severely limited in their usefulness"; and 2) that national forces impact state politics and that as a consequence
"states cannot usefully be viewed as political systems." Of
course, it is a *non-sequitur* to argue that because variance
among states or other aggregates is less than the variance
among individuals, the study of state politics is useless.
(Using Rose's logic, one might conclude that the study of
comparative government is also "severely limited in its usefulness" because the variance among individuals in the world
population is less than the variance among nations.) But it is
not the size of the variance that makes a topic theoretically
interesting; scholars study state politics because they are interested in explaining differences among states, however mo-

dest these differences may be in relation to differences among
individuals.

It is also a *non-sequitur* to argue that states "cannot usefully be viewed as political systems" because federal policy
affects the activity of states. We already know that federal
grants-in-aid affect state policy. But this does not render
systemic studies of state policy "useless." Indeed systemic
studies of the determinants of state policy are essential in
testing the influence of federal policy on state activities.
Virtually all of the relevant literature on the impact of federal policy in the states treat states as political systems responding to national policy.

Confusing Systemic and Incremental Models of
Policy Determination

Some years ago Charles Lindbloom observed that public
policy develops incrementally.[32] Decision makers do not an-
nually review the range of existing and proposed policies,
identify societal goals, research the benefits and costs of alternative policies in achieving these goals, rank preferences
for each alternative policy, and make a selection on the basis
of all relative information. They reduce their task by con-
sidering only *increments* of change proposed for next year in
programs, policies, and budgets. This descriptive model of
the policy-making process found in the writings of Lindbloom, Wildavsky, and Sharkansky is widely known as "incre-
mentalism."[33] Its utility in understanding the policy-making
process can hardly be overestimated. Anyone who has any
experience with state budget making can testify to its relevance. And there is comparative systematic evidence in support of incremental decision making. For example, the single
factor that shows the closest relationship to state government
expenditures in a current year are state government expenditures in the previous year. Indeed, current spending correlates

quite closely with expnditure levels in the states many decades
ago. Doubtless, current expenditure and service levels reflect
past habits, accommodations, and the conservative orientation
of government budget procedures. There is no question that
past decisions do have an important independent effect on
current decisions; and this fact helps to explain the relationship between past and previous expenditure levels.

Yet, it is important to realize that the incremental model
does not conflict with an economic resource model. Both explanatory models can be asserted simultaneously. To say
that public policies this year are related to public policies
last year does not contradict the statement that public policies this year *and* last year are a product of economic forces.
Both explanations are logically correct; they do not contradict each other.

Unfortunately, Ira Sharkansky offered the correlation between current and past expenditures as a refutation of the
economic model.[34] Sharkansky notes that current state government expenditures are more closely tied to previous state
government expenditures than to any socioeconomic or political variable. This is, of course, true. The problem is that he
asserts that this finding "contrasts" with those studies
showing the effect of economic resources. But actually the
correlation between past expenditures and present expenditures is shaped by the fact that the same environmental resources shape expenditures in both the present and the past.
For example, New York and Mississippi were at opposite
ends of the rank ordering of the states on levels of public
expenditures in the 1970's and the 1890's. During the same
periods, these states were also at the opposite ends of rank
ordering of the states on environmental resources. Their environmental resources shaped their relative expenditures in
both 1970 and 1890, so, of course there is a correlation between expenditures in these two long time periods.

It is logically incorrect to put previous expenditures together with current environmental conditions in a regression problem on current expenditures. This is because previous expenditures *embody* the effect of the environmental resources against which they are matched within the regression problem. On the basis of partial correlation coefficients in a multiple regression equation with both previous expenditures and current environmental resources, Sharkansky concluded that, "The impact of previous expenditures over current expenditures—the most noticeable in a multiple regression and partial correlation analysis with other independent variables. . . . indicates the great extent to which government expenditures depend upon intragovernmental stimuli rather than on economic, political, or social stimuli from their environment."[35] Economists were quick to note the logical confusion: Robert Harlow writes about Sharkansky's work: "Since . . . [environmental forces] were operative for 1961 as well, and since these factors are not likely to be radically different over the two-year span encompassed by the study, they are in a sense represented by, or contained in, the previous expenditure variable. . . . Using the previous expenditure variable tells us only that there are differences because there were differences."[36] Thus, economic and incremental explanations do not "contrast" with each other. They are both important contributions to our understanding of public policy.

Policy Innovation in the States

Another topic of interest in state policy research has been policy innovation. Policy innovation is simply the readiness of a government to adopt new programs and policies. Several years ago, Jack L. Walker constructed "an innovation score" for the American states based upon elapsed time between the first state adoption of a program and its later adoption by other states.[37] Walker monitored 88 different programs adopted by 20 or more states, and he averaged each state's score on each program adoption to produce an index of innovation for each state. The larger the innovation score, the faster the state had been in responding to new ideas or policies. Walker proceeded to explore relationships between these innovation scores of the fifty states and socioeconomic, political, and regional variables. It turned out the innovation was more readily accepted in the urban, industrialized, wealthy states.

However, in a subsequent study of policy innovation, Virginia Grey argued persuasively that no general tendency toward "innovativeness" really exists—that states that are innovative in one policy area are not necessarily the same states which are innovative in other areas.[38] She examined the adoption of 12 specific innovations in civil rights, welfare, and education, including the adoption of state public accommodations, fair housing, and fair employment laws, and merit systems and compulsory school attendance. States that were innovative in education were not necessarily innovative in civil rights or welfare. Nonetheless, she discovered that "first adopters" of most innovations tended to be wealthier states.

In short, studies of policy innovation suggest that innovation itself is linked to environmental resources. Wealth enables a state to afford the luxury of experimentation. In contrast, an absence of economic resources places constraints on the ability of the policy makers to raise revenue to pay for new programs or policies or to begin new undertakings. We can also imagine that urbanization would be conducive to policy innovation. Urbanization involves social change and creates demands for new programs and policies, and urbanization implies a concentration of creative resources in large cosmopolitan centers. Rural societies change less rapidly and are considered less adaptive and sympathetic to innovation. Finally, it is not unreasonable to expect that education should also facilitate innovation. An educated population should be more receptive toward innovation and public policy, and perhaps even more demanding of innovation. In summary, wealth, urbanization, and education, considered together, should provide a socioeconomic environment conducive to policy innovation.

Our own analysis of the relationship between environmental resources and innovation confirms this notion: Walker's innovation index for the states correlates income .56 with urbanization .54, and with education .32.[39]

We also believe that "professionalism" among both legislators and bureaucrats is a powerful stimulus to policy innovation. Professionalism involves, among other things, acceptance of professional reference groups as sources of information, standards, and norms. The professional bureaucrat attends national conferences, reads national journals, and perhaps aspires to build a professional reputation that extends beyond the boundaries of his own state. Thus, he constantly encounters new ideas, and he is motivated to pursue innovation for the purpose of distinguishing himself in his chosen field. Professionalism in legislatures involves reliance upon well-paid professional committee staff members who make it their business to keep up with the latest professional developments in the field of their committee's jurisdiction. The professional legislator knows about programatic developments in other states through professional meetings, journals, newsletters, etc. So we can expect measures of professionalism in both the executive and legislative branches of state government to be associated with policy innovation in the states.

It turns out that professionalism is indeed related to policy innovation. If we accept "civil service coverage" as a surrogate measure of professionalism in the bureacracy, and the "legislative professionalism scores" developed by the citizen's conference on state legislatures as surrogate measures of professionalism in state legislatures, we have some empirical evidence to support our notion that professionalism is an important contributor to policy innovation. The relationship between the innovation index and civil service coverage is .53 and the relationship between the innovation index and legislative professionalism is .62.

In summary, the explanation of policy innovation appears to be one that emphasizes professionalism in legislatures and bureaucracies, as well as wealth, education, and urbanization as an environmental setting.

Policy Analysis: Capitalistic and Communist Nations

Findings in American states that pluralist political variables—particularly competition, participation, and equity in representation—do not count for much in determining levels of taxing, spending, benefits, and services, are ideologically discomforting for many political scientists. How far can we go in asserting the proposition that *democratic pluralism* is not really an important determinant to public policy? Can we hypothesize that the structure of *national* political systems is not really relevant to the level of benefits and services provided to their citizens? Is it possible that democratic *nations* do not produce noticeably different levels of public spending, services, and benefits than non-democratic nations at the same level of economic development? For example, is it possible that welfare benefits and social security programs in communist nations are the same as those in capitalistic nations with similar economic resources? Is it possible that educational benefits and services in capitalistic

and communistic nations with similar economic resources
are equivalent? Is it possible that environmental resources,
rather than the extent of democracy in the political system,
are really the determining forces in shaping public policy in
nations of the world?

Despite the obvious importance of these questions, systematic cross-national research on public policy is relatively
rare in political science. Only recently have political scientists in the field of comparative government actually begun
to make systematic comparisons of the levels of taxing,
spending, benefits, and services among nations.

One of the first studies to tackle these kinds of questions
from a cross-national perspective is Phillips Cutright's study
of social security programs in 76 nations.[10] Cutright examined
national social insurance programs in terms of the extent of
coverage in the level of benefits in work injury programs,
sickness and maternity programs, old age invalidism and
death insurance programs, family allowance plans, and un-
employment programs. He also examined "political representativeness" in order to assess the importance of democracy
in the political system to the social security and welfare programs provided to national populations. His hypothesis, of
course, was "that governments in nations whose political
structures tend to allow for greater assessability to the people
of the governing elite will act to provide greater social security for their population than that provided by governments whose rulers are less assessable to the demands of the
population." Such a hypothesis fits neatly with democratic
political theory.

But it turned out that political representativeness had
relatively little effect on national social security and welfare
programs. In spite of very great differences among nations in
ideological orientation and type of political system, social
security and welfare programs are closely related to levels

of economic development. Indeed, Cutright reports that energy consumption by itself accounts for 81% of the variation among nations in the extent of coverage and level of benefits provided by national social insurance and welfare programs. Similar social security and welfare programs are found in democratic and non-democratic nations with the same levels of economic development. His findings directly challenged traditional democratic pluralist political wisdom:

> A government can act without being told what to do. The scholar operating within a democratic context (and especially that of the United States) may tend to view government activities as being dependent upon the demands of secondary groups. A major but tentative conclusion that can be drawn from this study of government activity is that it need not await the petition of secondary groups. The role (or even the existence) of politically relevant secondary groups in guiding government decisions in many of the nations included in this study is modest.
>
> In many nations we would conclude that the introduction of social security measures is a response by government to changes in the economic and social order that is not strongly affected by some degree of departure from ideal organizational forms. Similar levels of social security coverage are found in nations whose governments are thought to act in response to the popular will as occur in nations whose governments are thought to act with less regard to public demand. It appears that the level of social security in a nation is a response to deeper strains affecting the organization of society. Governments may ignore human needs, but there are rather tight limits on the extent to which they may ignore organizational requirements.[41]

It should be noted here that Professor Cutright is a sociologist and not a political scientist.

Another important, systematic, cross-national policy study

is economist Frederic L. Pryor's *Public Expenditures in Communist and Capitalist Nations.*[42] Pryor examined expenditures for national security, internal security, education, health, welfare, science, interest and investment, and administration, in six communist and six capitalist nations. In generalizing from a myriad of findings, Pryor concluded that communist and capitalist political systems provide essentially the same types and levels of public expenditures, benefits, and services for their citizens.

In an interpretation of his own findings Pryor observed:

> Such results can be interpreted in several ways. They suggest to me that the policy dilemmas facing decision-makers of public consumption expenditures are quite similar in all nations, regardless of system. Such policy problems include: the desirability of financing a service through the public rather than the private sector; the proper relationship of different public consumption expenditures to the tax revenues which must be raised; in balancing citizen's demand for particular services with the adjudged interests of the state. If the basic economic circumstances (in Marxist terminology 'productive forces') are similar and if the policy dilemmas are similar, it should not be surprizing that the decisions are also roughly similar. . .
>
> It should not be surprising with the decline of ideological dogmatism since the early Cold War years, the similarity of public consumption expenditures in nations with different economic systems has been increasingly recognized by economists in both east and west. . .
>
> As a study between market and centrally planned economies, one important conclusion fans out: in regard to public consumption expenditures there are few essential differences between nations of the two systems, at least on the macro-economic level on which the analysis is carried out. . .
>
> Difficulties abound, of course, in making comparison be-

tween nations with different economic systems, and on a number of specific points we must be content with only first approximation. But it should be evident that sufficient information is available for systematic comparisons to be made, and, with the rising quantity in quality of data being published by all nations, such work is becoming easier to carry out with every passing year. Thus we are gradually receiving the proper information to separate propaganda from reality and to isolate the actual rather than the theoretical differences between economic systems. Of course, decisions-makers in each nation have certain vested interests in publicizing the merits of their own particular economic institutions. But scholars should be able to penetrate such rationalizations through a comparative analysis of special aspects of these economies.[43]

Despite these generalizations, however, Pryor recognized the influence of some "political" factors in determining certain expenditure patterns. For example, regarding health and welfare programs, Pryor found that the date of the introduction of the social insurance system correlated with the political mobilization of workers, as reflected in the growth of unionization. However, once social insurance programs were introduced, they appeared to expand incrementally in both communist and capitalistic countries.

Sociologist Harold L. Wilensky contributed to the growing body of cross-national policy research in his study of the determinants of *The Welfare State and Equality*. Wilensky's conclusion that economic development "is the root cause of welfare state development"[44] again challenges the assumptions of many political scientists that political system characteristics and elite ideology *must* determine welfare policy. According to Wilensky, political systems (e.g. "liberal democratic" versus "equal opportunity") are "weak predictors" of spending efforts in national social security programs. He con-

firms the findings of Cutright, Pryor, and others that nations
at the same level of economic development provide roughly
the same levels and types of social security and welfare services, whether these nations are socialist or capitalist, democratic or totalitarian, collectivist or individualist According to Wilensky, economic development affects the proportion of aged in the population, as well as the age of the social
security program itself; and these three variables together explain 83 percent of the variance among nations in the proportion of the GNP devoted to social welfare. "There is not
much variance left to explain" (p. 47). The addition of political system characteristics and elite ideology fail to increase
the explained variance.

These general conclusions are based on multiple regression
and path analytical models applied to cross-sectional data
on 64 countries. But what if economic development, age of
population, and age of system are "controlled," and we examine only the twenty-two wealthiest countries for which
time-series data are available? Wilensky hypothesizes that
diversity among these wealthy nations in social security programs may be based upon governmental centralization, social
heterogeneity, occupational mobility, methods of financing
social security, and the extent of working class organization.
He cites individual cases to support these hypotheses, but he
scrupulously notes contradictions as well. For example, six of
the nine welfare state "leaders" are among the nine most
centralized governments; among the seven welfare "laggards," four are among the least centralized. Thus, if we are
willing to "control" for economic development and accept
less rigorous observations about differences between "leaders" and "laggards," we can still salvage some limited "political" hypotheses about the determinants of welfare programs. Later in the volume, however, Professor Wilensky
offers more convincing explanations of differences in welfare

programs among the wealthy nations: a tendency toward specialization in types of social service programs which is rooted in historical experiences. For example, the neglect of national health programs in some nations (U.S., Canada, Austrailia) may be linked to a heavy investment in higher education; while heavy spending on pensions may bring neglect of higher education (Austria, Italy).

Some other interesting questions posed by Wilensky: Is military spending greater among capitalist nations than socialist nations? Does heavy military spending dampen social security development? It turns out that "military spending as a fraction of the GNP is uncorrelated with either types of political system or level of economic develpoment." Big wars and large scale mobilization turn out to be "oddly egalitarian," not only because they bring full employment and capacity production, but also because crisis itself seems to "inspire a collective willingness to move fast in the development of the welfare state." Cross-sectional data indicates that military operation is irrelevant to social security spending; but time-series data on wealthy nations suggests that the Cold War of the 1950's depressed welfare spending in these nations.

The notion that political considerations may be influential in policy innovation, particularly in health and welfare programs, is well argued by Arnold J. Heidenheimer in an essay comparing social policy development in western Europe and the United States.[45] He argues that conservative regimes —Prussia and Austria—first introduced social insurance on paternalistic principles. But liberal governments did not introduce social insurance programs until after the unionization of their work forces. He concludes that "the timing of the introduction of public pensions seem to have been determined by complex relationships between the growth of labor unions, the prevailing ideologies, and the strategies of social demand anticipation on the part of governments." He argues that the working classes in America are concentrated on education as an instrument of social mobility, while the working classes in Europe backed social insurance and welfare programs as an instrument of social equality. These differences in political objectives and strategies, he believes, accounts for the fact that the American educational system is "ahead" of European systems of education, while the U.S. health and welfare programs are "behind" comparable to European ones.

Thus most comparative cross-national policy studies indicate that health and welfare policies, regardless of political systems, are closely associated with levels of economic development. However, some studies suggest that diversity in political systems do create some programmatic differences, independent of the availability of resources; but these differences appear to center about the time of adoption of particular programs and the type of program emphasis. The emerging field of cross-national policy research offers excitement and challenge to political scientists interested in systematic policy analysis.

Democracy and Policy Responsiveness

Are democratic political systems more *responsive* to socioeconomic conditions than non-democratic systems? A common belief of traditional democratic-pluralist ideology is that competitive, participatory, repesentative political systems —pluralistic democracies—are the more responsive in policy decisions to the social and economic conditions affecting their citizens. Presumably, pluralistic democracies—with competitive parties, widespread participation, and representative institutions—extend influence to broader sectors of the population. This widening of the influence is supposed to result in a greater tendency to enact the preferences of lower strata of the population into public policy. Thus, among pluralistic democracies, we would expect to find greater congruence between characteristics of the population and public policy than among non-democratic political systems. In short, democratic political sytems should be more responsive to socioeconomic conditions affecting their populations than non-democratic systems.

To test these notions about the greater responsiveness of democratic political systems, we can divide nations into those which are democratic and those which are not, and then observe whether there is a closer relationship between socioeconomic conditions affecting the population and public policies in democratic nations than in non-democratic nations. Ideally, we would expect to find closer relationships in democratic nations than in non-democratic nations.

But surprisingly the results of systematic analysis are just the *reverse* of what we would expect on the basis of a priori reasoning from democratic theory. It turns out that relationships between socioeconomic characteristics of national populations and public policies of these nations are closer among communist nations and autocracies than among democratic nations.[46] Political scientist Larry Wade provides data showing that per capita income is *less* related to health, education, and welfare measures in affluent democracies than in poor democracies or communist nations or autocracies.*

---

*His affluent democracies were the United States, Sweden, Switzerland, Canada, Iceland, Denmark, Australia, France, New Zealand, Luxemburg, Belgium, the United Kingdom, West Germany, Finland, and the Netherlands. His communist states were East Germany, Czechoslovakia, the USSR, Poland, Hungary, Rumania, Bulgaria, Yugoslavia, Cuba, Albania, and China. His poor democracies were Israel, Austria, Italy, Japan, Ireland, Uruguay, Malta, Mexico, Jamaica, Costa Rica, Lebanon, Colombia, the Philippines, Ceylon, and India. His autocracies

For example, per capita income explains over 20 percent of the variation in higher education enrollment in communist countries and poor democracies, and 40 percent of the variation in autocracies, but only 6 percent of the variation in higher education enrollments in the affluent, western democracies. Per capita income explains 72 percent of the variation in physician services among poorer democracies, 26 percent among communist nations, 37 percent among autocracies, but only 16 percent of the variation in physician services among affluent western democracies. The same differences between democratic and non-democratic nations and communist and non-communist nations can be observed in other policy areas. In short, available evidence runs contrary to the proposition that policy outcomes and socioeconomic conditions affecting the population are more closely related in democratic than in non-democratic nations.

Let us pursue the same notion about the greater responsiveness of democratic-pluralist political systems in the American states. We can divide states into those which are more pluralist—states with competitive parties and high voter turnout—and those which are not so pluralist—states with one party system and low voter turnout. We can then observe whether there is a closer relationship between socioeconomic conditions and public policy in pluralist states than in the non-pluralist states. On the basis of all priority reasoning from pluralist political theory we would expect to find closer relationships between socioeconomic conditions and public policies are closer in the non-pluralist states than in the pluralist states. For example, median family income explains

were Kuwait, Spain, Portugal, South Africa, Nicaragua, Saudi Arabia, El Salvador, Iran, Peru, Jordan, Domincan Republic, Taiwan, Honduras, Paraguay, Bolivia, Liberia, Thailand, Indonesia, Pakistan, South Vietnam, Sudan, Nepal, Haiti, Burma, Afghanistan, and Ethiopia.

only 25 percent of the variance in per pupil expenditures among pluralist states, compared to 64 percent of the variance in per pupil expenditures for non-pluralist states. Median family income explains only 20 percent of the variance in welfare benefits among pluralist states, compared to 65 percent of the variance in welfare benefits among non-pluralist states. This same pattern holds true for other policy measures as well.

In short, there is no empirical evidence that democratic nations are any more responsive to socioeconomic forces which affect their citizens than non-democratic nations, or that pluralist states are any more responsive to socioeconomic conditions affecting their citizens than non-pluralist states.

I am not prepared to argue on the basis of these limited findings that non-democratic nations and non-pluralist states are *more* responsive than democratic nations and pluralist states. My own guess is that the apparent greater responsiveness of non-democratic nations and non-pluralist states is really a product of economic underdevelopment. The democratic nations and pluralistic states are generally affluent. This affluence relieves them from some of the constraints of limited economic resources. Once a certain level of affluence is attained, non-economic forces probably play a greater role in the determination of public policy. In contrast, less affluent nations and states are heavily constrained by the availability of economic resources. A high level of economic development provides decision-makers with greater latitude in policy choices, and tends to free them from restraints imposed by limited resources. Thus, policy measures are closely related to economic variables in poor nations and states, but less closely related to economic variables among more affluent nations and states.

Conclusion

This brief survey of the policy research literature on states and nations was not designed to demonstrate the merits of economic determinism. Instead, it was designed to challenge political scientists to reexamine many of their professional predispositions and ideological commitments, and to stimulate the development of a geniune policy science. Policy research is still very exploratory; no body of literature can be thought of as "the final word" in understanding public policy. But systematic policy research to date is sufficiently challenging to the traditional professional concerns of political science, and to the long standing assumptions of democratic pluralist ideology, to warrant a serious reconsideration of the traditional assumptions of our discipline.

TABLE 1

THE RELATIONSHIPS BETWEEN INCOME
AND HEALTH AND EDUCATION MEASURES IN
DEMOCRATIC AND NON-DEMOCRATIC NATIONS

	Amount of Variance Explained by Per Capita Income			
	Physicians per 10,000	Hospital Beds per 10,000	Male Life Expectancy	Enroll. Higher Ed.
Affluent Democracies	16%	0%	9%	6%
Poorer Democracies	72	13	64	21
Communist Nations	26	83	42	20
Autocracy	37	6	41	40

Source: Derived from figures supplied by Larry L. Wade, *The Elements of Public Policy* (Columbus: Charles T. Merrill, 1972). Tables 2.2, 2.3, 2.4.
Original data from United Nations, *Statistical Yearbook 1968* and *Yearbook of National Accounts and Statistics 1969*.

TABLE 2

THE RELATIONSHIPS BETWEEN INCOME AND WELFARE AND EDUCATION MEASURES IN PLURALIST AND NON-PLURALIST STATES

	Amount of Variance Explained by Median Family Income			
	Per Pupil Expenditures	AFDC Benefits	Per Capita Taxes	Police Protection
Pluralist States	25%	20%	35%	
Non-Pluralist States	64%	65%	70%	

Source: Data from *Statistical Abstract of the United States, 1972.*

3 POLICY ANALYSIS: AMERICAN CITIES

Comparative, systematic research on public policy in American cities is relatively recent. Most of the early research on municipal government was prescriptive and noncomparative. Case studies of policy issues, in particular cities, were commonplace; and there was a great deal of literature prescribing for the ills of urban life—advocating "reforms" and "solutions" of various sorts. But systematic comparisons of the policies of different cities, and careful analysis of the causes and consequences of policy differences, is relatively rare in the political science literature on municipal government.

Reformism in American Cities

The best comparative research on American cities in political science focuses on the instituional structure of municipal government. The reform movement in municipal politics promoted a series of structural "reforms"—including the manager rather than the mayor form of government, non-partisan rather than partisan elections, and at-large rather than ward election districts. Early writings in municipal government simply extolled the virtues of these "good government" reforms without systematically examining the linkage between these structures and either environmental conditions or policy consequences.

However, the behavioral movement turned the attention of several scholars to the social, economic, and political forces affecting the success of the reform movement and shaping the structure of city government. Studies by John Kessel, Edgar Sherbenou, Phillips Cutright, Robert Alford, and Harry Scoble, in the early 1960's, provided the first systematic, comparative view of the linkage between the urban environment and the structure of city politics.[1] These scholars reported that the more "political" form of mayor-council government, in contrast to the more "efficient" form of council-manager government, was more likely to be found in large cities in the East and Midwest with heavy proportions of working class residents, low income families, and ethnic minorities. The manager form of government was found to be associated with middle-sized, white collar, well-educated, non-ethnic populations The non-partisan ballot was more likely to be adopted in the homogeneous middle-class cities where there was less social cleavage and smaller proportions of working class ethnic group members. Partisan ballots were the prevailing style of local elections in large Eastern cities with large ethnic populations and heavy blue-collar employment.

In reviewing this literature on the linkage between the urban environment and the structure of city government, political scientist Brett W. Hawkins concluded:

> Clearly the most frequent pattern relates to the political impact of social differences among people. Indicators of ethnic, religious, and life-style differences are associated with the retention of unreformed, politicized, group arbitrating forms—including decentralized, fragmented govern-

ments. The same is true where the local economy, sub-communities, population size, and population's stability suggest more human diversity and a cementing a people's socioeconomic ties to the community.[2]

Sociologists Alford and Scoble reached the same conclusions:

> Social heterogeneity—the existence of sizable groups with diverse political cultures and demands—favors a more "politicized," less centralized, less professionalized form because there is not as great a consensus among politically active groups upon the proper goals of city government and a greater need for access and representation from diverse groups. A relatively high proportion of middle-class persons favors a less politicized form because such groups are less likely to have political demands inconsistent with the centralized, efficient form. Population growth and mobility favor a less politicized form because cities are facing new problems requiring administrative and managerial skills, at the same time that a low proportion of the population is settled into stable social and political groups.[3]

Of course caution is in order; there are always exceptions and these relationships are not so close as to permit accurate prediciton of political system characteristics by simply knowing the characteristics of the environment.

Economic Determinants of City Policies

Economists led the way in systematic research on the determinants of municipal policy. In 1959 economists Harvey Brazer compared the spending patterns of 462 cities of 25,000 or more in the United States.[4] He examined the determinants not only of total general expenditures, but also expenditures for police protection, fire protection, highways, recreation, sanitation, general control, etc. He identified a number of

environmental conditions which increased per capita levels
of public spending in cities: population density, median
family income, inter-governmental revenues, population size,
population growth rate, manufacturing, trade, and service
employment. Of these characteristics, the most influential
were population density, median family income, and inter-
governmental revenue. An increase in any of these factors
leads to an increase in city taxing, spending, and service
levels. We might consider population density, size, and
growth rate as measures of *demands*; and median family
income, intergovernmental revenue, and employment as
measures of *resources*.

In recent years a growing volume of economic research
has centered on the linkage between the urban environment and the taxing and spending policies of cities.[5] These
studies (many appearing in the *National Tax Journal, American Economic Review*, and *Municipal Finance*) tended to
focus on five somewhat interrelated topics: (1) the relationship between taxing and spending and economic resources
and fiscal capacity; (2) the relationship between taxing and
spending and demands associated with characteristics of urban populations; (3) the economies and dis-economies of
scale in providing public services; and (4) the fiscal burdens
and benefits of political fragmentation in metropolitan areas;
(5) the relationship between city taxing and spending and
aid received from higher levels of government.

The economic *resources* identified as particularly important determinants of city taxing and spending were per capita and median family income, property value per capita, and
measures of manufacturing and trade. Interestingly, the most
important measure of *demand* reflected in demographic characteristics of the city population was population density: it
turns out that levels of taxing, spending, benefits, and services in cities, increase with increases in population density.

Other measures of demand included the proportion of the population which is non-white, the mobility of the population, crowding within a dwelling unit, the percentage of the population of foreign stock, and age charactesistics of the population. It turned out that environmental resources and demands were very successful in explaining city expenditures in several policy areas, notably police, fire protection, sanitation, and streets. Frequently researchers reported explained variances ranging from 40 percent to 75 percent in these common functions of city governments. (See Table 3-1).

Another finding reported in this research was that the ratio of central city to metropolitan area population also affected city taxing, spending, and services.[6] The smaller the city in relation to its metropolitan area, the higher the taxes, spending, and service costs of that city. This suggests that cities with large suburban rings are bearing the burdens imposed by suburban populations who use city services.

Research on the impact of federal aid on city policy suggests that this aid is a positive stimulus to increases in spending and services.[7] More importantly, there is no evidence to support the notion that federal aid replaces local tax effort. On the contrary, increases in federal aid tend to increase local expenditures not only for the aided functions but for non-aided functions as well. Federal aid increases *city spending* not only in the areas aided by the federal government but in non-aided areas as well.

In a careful analysis of the taxing and spending patterns of both cities and suburbs in metropolitan areas, economist Woo Sik Kee identified the differentials in burdens and benefits between city and suburban governments.[8] Suburban governments spent more per capita and per pupil for education than city governments. City governments spent more per capita than suburbs for poverty linked functions—public welfare,

TABLE 3

EXPLAINED VARIATION IN MUNICIPAL SPENDING
FOR POLICE, FIRE, SANITATION, AND STREETS

Study	Explained Variance (R^2) (Numbers of significant independent variables in parenthesis)			
	Police	Fire	Sanitation	Streets
Brazer	.26 (5)	.27 (4)	.10 (3)	.16 (3)
Bahl	.64 (9)	.51 (7)	.29 (1)	.27 (3)
Weicher	.73 (12)	.64 (15)	.32 (4)	.34 (5)
Adams	.75 (9)	.65 (10)	.55 (9)	.42 (6)
Pidot	.76 (3)	.66 (3)	.53 (3)	.27 (2)

health and hospital services, and educational expenditures
for children in poverty impacted families. Cities also spend
more than suburbs for common municipal functions—police,
fire, sanitation, recreation, and general control. General fiscal
burdens were greater in cities than in suburbs (general fiscal burden was defined as general revenues minus intergovernmental receipts divided by income). Tax burdens in cities were also greater than the tax burdens in suburbs (the
tax burden was defined as the total of taxes divided by income). Because Professor Kee was dealing with cities of
roughly comparable functions, he was able to explain a very
high proportion of variation in total general expenditures as
well as expenditures for education, highways, health, hospi-
tals, and welfare in these cities. Indeed, he was able to explain 70 to 85 percent of the variance in city expenditures,
total and by function. His explanatory variables were per
capita income, state aid, ratio of central city population to
the SMSA population, homeownership, and population density. He concludes with observation that changes in the social, economic, and demographic variables may indeed account for future changes in taxing, spending, and benefits in

central cities. But these variables, he notes, cannot be *manipulated* by public policy because they are largely determined by forces outside the realm of governmental control. On the other hand, the major factor associated with variations in city policy which *can* be influenced by government was the ratio of central city population to SMSA population and to per capita state and federal aid.

Economists were also the first social scientists to examine the linkage between the form of government in cities and taxing and spending policies. Economist Bernard H. Booms asked whether manager or mayor forms of government had any influence on the level of public taxing and spending.[9] He examined the form of government and taxing and spending in 73 cities in Ohio and Michigan. He observed significantly lower per capita public expenditure in manager cities in relation to mayor cities. However, he did not inquire as to whether these mayor and manager cities differed in socioeconomic composition. Indeed, Booms suggested that the impact of environmental variables would be an important question for "future research."

One of the first important studies of municipal public policy by political scientists was a study by Oliver P. Williams which attempted to classify cities according to the types of policies their citizens and officials expected of them.[10] Williams developed a typology of four different roles for local government: (1) promoting economic growth; (2) providing for life's amenities; (3) maintaining public services, that is, a caretaker role; and (4) arbitrating among conflicting interests. The community whose major concern is promoting economic growth is prepared to enact zoning regulations, reduce tax assessments, develop industrial parks, install utilities, and do whatever else may be required to attract business and industry. A community concerned with securing life's amenities adopts policies which are designed to protect the

home environment rather than the working environment
—laws stressing safety, slowness, quiet, beauty, convenience,
and restfulness. Heavy industry is excluded and population
growth discouraged. He observes that middle and upper income residential suburbs in large metropolitan areas are
likely to be amenity communities. The caretaker government,
on the other hand, is expected to provide minimal public services, and keep tax burdens low. Caretaker policies are pre-
ferred in small cities serving rural areas and in working class
communities composed of homeowners who can barely afford
the home they are buying and do not want to pay taxes for
amenities of any kind. An arbiter government is primarily
concerned with managing conflicts among competing interests and finding workable compromises that can be enac-
ted in the public policy. An arbiter goverment is more likely
to be found in large heterogeneous communities, where social
and economic cleavages create demands for different policies, rather than in a homgeneous community, where there is
substantial agreement on the proper policies for government
to follow.

Some studies have examined specific public policies in a
limited number of cities. Sociologist Terry N. Clark studied
urban renewal policy in 51 cities and concluded that urban
renewal activity correlated with population size, community
poverty, religion (Catholic), and education.[11] I studied educational policy in 67 cities and found that population size was
associated with racial segregation in public schools.[12] Examination of both teacher and pupil segregation revealed that
larger cities (especially in the North) are more segregated
than the smaller ones. In a separate study, I found that population size is also related to educational policy outcomes in
large cities.[13] Per pupil expenditures in city schools are related to size, income, and property value; per pupil expenditures are negatively associated with the size of the non-

white population. Similar relationships were observed for teacher salaries, teacher-pupil ratios, and other educational policy measures. In another study, I found that class and life-style differences were associated with different policy choices in 5 Wisconsin central cities and their 38 suburbs. Higher status, family centered suburbs were found to spend more money per child on education than central cities, at least in larger metropolitan areas. However in smaller metropolitan areas where class differences between cities and suburbs were not so great, there was less differential in educational expenditures between cities and suburbs.

What generalizations can be derived about studies of the linkage between the urban environment and public policy? Generally, the research suggests most clearly that environment is a major determinant of public policy. This is true whether policy is measured strictly in terms of city taxing and spending patterns, public benefits and services, or policy typologies. In reviewing the literature linking urban environment to city policies, political scientist Brett W. Hawkins concludes: " . . .large and dense populations and large minority (racial, religious, and ethnic) subpopulations correlate with general city spending and spending for specific purposes. These correlations, while not uniform, suggest that larger, denser, and more heterogeneous environments generate demands for services by various segments of the population and that city goverments often respond favorably to these demands."[15]

Reformism and Public Policy

Traditionally, political scientists assumed that the reform of the political system in American cities would bring about changes in public policy. The reform of municipal government was expected to result in better public services, lower

tax rates, more efficient cost-benefit ratios, and more professional administration. Of course, it was natural for reform-
oriented political scientists to *assume* that what they were
studying was important—manager versus mayor government,
partisan versus non-partisan elections, the powers of mayors
and councils, home rule, etc. Yet assumptions about the importance of structural reforms are no substitute for the systematic investigation of the actual linkages between political
system characteristics and public policies.

It is no easy task to demonstrate the *independent* effect of
political system characteristics on city politics. It is difficult
to sort out the policy differences which can be attributed to
governmental reform from the policy differences which are
a function of the socioeconomic character of city populations.
In general, political scientists have found it difficult to dis-
cover political system characteristics that explain variation
in city policies independently of the effects of urban enviroment.

One explicit use of the systems model for sorting out the
effect of environmental variables on public policy from the
effect of governmental reform is found in the study by Chester B. Rogers of city expenditure patterns in all cities with a
population of 25,000 or more. According to Rogers:

> The [systems] model specifies three sets of variables for
> consideration: the political system, its environment, and its
> outputs. According to it, the determinants of city govern-
> ment outputs or policies can be found either in the political
> system or in the environment. Like all models it is a simpli-
> fication of reality, thus omits some factors; but it does pro-
> vide a framework for developing hypotheses about policy
> determinants.[16]

Rogers found that the most important determinants of per
capita expenditures, total and by function, were: population

density; familism(the fertility rate, the women in the work force, and single family housing); and population mobility. These measures appear to reflect *demands* rather than *resources* of urban populations. Rogers found that resource measures—median family income, affluence, property value —were not closely related to expenditure levels.

But his findings regarding *political* system characteristics were even more important. Rogers did *not* find any significant relationship between form of government, partisan or non-partisan elections, or ward or at-large constituencies, and municipal taxing and spending patterns. There were some differences between the means on spending measures of reformed and unreformed governments, but these differences were attributed to differences in the socioeconomic characteristics of reformed and unreformed cities. Rogers concluded:

> One of the most obvious findings of the study is that none of the political variables considered had an influence on the policy. In every case either there was no significant relationship between political and policy measures, or in those cases where a significant relationship was found, additional analysis indicated it to be a function of both variables being related to an environmental variable.[17]

In contrast, several studies have attempted to show some kind of relationship between reformism and city policy. Political scientist George S. Duggar reports that mayor cities are quicker to respond to the lure of federal money than manager cities and that mayor cities got a faster start under urban renewal programs.[18] On the other hand, Duggar reports that once urban renewal programs were begun, manager cities experienced slightly greater program achivement than mayor cities. However, Duggar admits that population size is a more influential variable in urban renewal achievement than governmental structure: greater achievement is associated with greater size.

The structure of city governments was also found to be related to outcomes in water fluoridation battles. In the comparative study of several hundred cities, sociologist Robert L. Crane and Donald D. Rosenthal found that fluoridation had a better chance of consideration and adoption in cities having the strong executive—either a manager or a strong partisan mayor.[19] The absence of strong executive leadership frequently spelled the need for fluoridation. Another structural variable—partisanship—was also related to fluoridation outcomes. In both mayor and manager cities, partisan electoral systems were associated with greater adoptions of fluoridation laws by city councils.

In summarizing the literature dealing with the relationships between city political systems and public policies, Brett W. Hawkins concludes:

> The studies described here show that system has a policy impact, but that *none of them shows that system variables have a bigger impact than environmental variables*. However, many studies do demonstrate that *system is important to policy explanation simultaneously with environmental factors*. Urban renewal, enforcement of traffic laws, flouridation, school desegregation, policy treatment of juvenile offenders, wage garnishment legislation, stages of policy development, and per capita expenditures for services—all of these are to some degree shaped by system variables.[20] [Italics mine]

But in general, the research on the relationships between the structure of city government and the content of public policy again challenges the professional and ideological assumptions of political scientists that govermental structure must impact public policy. Governmental structure *may* affect the content of policy. But the burden of proof is on those who assert such a relationship. We cannot promise citizens or decision-makers that tinkering with the structure of their government is going to bring about significant policy changes.

Reformism and Policy Responsiveness

Perhaps the most important systematic study of policy consequences of reformism is a comprehensive analysis of the taxing and spending policies of 200 American cities of 50,000 or more by political scientists Robert L. Lineberry and Edmond D. Fowler.[21] They found that reformed cities tended to tax and spend *less* than unreformed cities. Cities with manager governments and at-large council constituencies were *less* willing to spend money for public purpose than cities with mayor-council governments and ward constituencies. (Cities with partisan elections, however, did not actually spend any more than cities with non-partisan elections.) In short, reformism *does* save tax money.

Lineberry and Fowler also found that environmental variables had an important impact on tax and spending policies. For example, they concluded that:

1. The more middle class the city, measured by income, education, and occupation, the lower the general tax and spending levels.

2. The greater the homeownership in a city, the lower the tax and spending levels.

3. The larger the percentage of religious and ethnic minorities in the population, the higher the city's taxes and expenditures.

What turned out to be an even more important finding in

the Lineberry and Fowler study was the difference in *responsiveness* of the two kinds of city governments—reformed and unreformed—to the socioeconomic composition of their populations. These researchers simply grouped their cities into subsamples—reformed cities (cities with manager governments, non-partisan elections, and at-large constituencies) and unreformed cities (cities with mayor-council governments, partisan elections, and ward constituencies). Among reformed cities there was no significant correlations between tax and spending policies and income and educational, occupational, religious, and ethnic characteristics of their population. In contrast, among unreformed cities there

TABLE 4

ENVIRONMENTAL CHARACTERISTICS AND
TAX AND SPENDING POLICY IN
REFORMED AND UNREFORMED CITIES

Relationship Between	Correlation Between Environmental Characteristics and Taxing and Spending	
	Reformed Cities	Unreformed Cities
TAXES and		
Ethnicity	.62	.34
Private school attendance	.40	.25
Homeownership	−.70	−.44
Education	−.55	−.13
EXPENDITURES and		
Ethnicity	.51	.05
Private school attendance	.46	.08
Homeownership	−.67	−.38
Education	−.49	−.37

Source: Adapted from figures in Robert L. Lineberry and Edmund P. Fowler, "Reformism and Public Policy in American Cities," *American Political Science Review*, 61 (September 1967), 701–716.

were many significant correlations between taxing and spending policies and these socioeconomic characteristics of the population.

They concluded that reformism tends to reduce the importance of class, homeownership, ethnicity, and religion in city politics. It tends to minimize the role that social conflicts play in public decision making. In contrast, mayor-council governments, ward constituencies, and partisan elections permit social cleavages to be reflected in city politics and public policy to be responsive to socioeconomic factors. These findings suggest that reformed cities have gone a long way toward accomplishing the reformist goal; that is, "to immunize city governments from 'artificial' social cleavages —race, religion, ethnicity, and so on." Thus, political institutions seem to play an important role in policy formation:

> . . .a role substantially independent of a city's demography. . . . Non-partisan elections, at-large constituencies, and manager governments are associated with a lessened responsiveness of cities to the enduring conflicts of political life.

Policy Innovation in Communities

Community policy "innovation" in public housing and urban renewal was examined by sociologists Micheal Aiken and Robert Alford in comparative analyses of over 600 cities.[23] These researchers posited three measures of community "innovation": the presence or absence of public housing or urban renewal programs; the speed of adoption as measured by the number of years after the passage of federal aid legislation that the community began its first project; and the level of output measures in terms of the number of housing units constructed per 100,000 population.

A wide variety of independent variables were tested as

possible determinants of these measures of community "innovation" in public housing and urban renewal. Aiken and Alford did not classify their independent variables in terms of economic resources or needs, or directly test economic versus political explanation of innovation. However, their variables included measures of community *resources* (median family income, adult population with high school education); community *needs* (percent of housing which is dilapidated, percent of families in poverty, adult population with less than five years of schooling, percent unemployed); *racial and ethnic composition* (percent nonwhite, percent foreign born); *size and age* of city; and *political structure* (form of government, type of election, type of constituency).

It turned out that measures of community *need* were more closely associated with policy innovation in public housing and urban renewal than any other condition. "Cities with more dilapidated housing, many poor families, many poorly educated adults, more high school dropouts, and many nonwhites were indeed more likely to have entered the public housing program, entered it faster, and have higher performance levels." These relationships held up under statistical controls.

It is not surprising that community needs correlate with policy innovation. What might surprise politcal scientists, however, is that policy in public housing and urban renewal was found to be either completely *un*related to political and structural variables or very weakly related to them. Form of government (mayor council versus council manager), type of election (partisan versus nonpartisan), type of constituency (ward versus at-large), percent voting Democratic, and percent voter turnout, were all *less* closely associated with community policy innovation than measures of community need. In their conclusions Aiken and Alford "suggest" that organizational structure and professionalism may contribute to policy innovation, but they admit to having "no direct measures of these properties."

The Threads of Public Policy

Reserch on the determinants of public policy in cities has focused our attenion on the relationships between environmental resources (and needs) and public policy. But we also want to know what happens *within* political systems. How does the system go about transferring demands originating from the environment into public policies?

Comparative analysis which reveals relationships between urban resources or needs and public policy is vitally important in the development of a policy science, but it does not really tell us much about what goes on inside the urban political system. To cite an analogy: finding a high correlation between cigarette smoking and the incidence of cancer among humans is important; but this correlation does not in itself reveal the functioning of cells within the human body. We still want to know *how* human cancers are formed and how they behave. So also finding a high correlation between population density and spending for police protection does not in itself reveal the functioning of urban political systems. We still want to know *how* a city's political system goes about transforming demands arising from the environment into public policy.

Perhaps the most comprehensive study of what goes on *within* a city's governmental structure, notably within the the city council, is the Stanford University City Council Research Project—a comparative study of 82 city councils in the San Francisco Bay region, directed by Heinz Eulau. The Project has already produced numerous articles and six books, including the summary volume *Labyrinths of Democracy: Adaptations, Linkages, Representation, and Policies in*

Urban Politics, with still more to come.[24] As important as this work is in the study of municipal government, its central focus is not the explanation of urban public policy, but rather an examination of local representation, council-constituency linkages, and councilmanic decision-making. Nonetheless, public policy is not ignored; on the contrary, according to Eulau, "the test of a governing body's responsiveness is, ultimately, in the kinds of politics it pursues—that is, in the ways in which it commits the community."[25]

In *Labyrinths of Democracy*, Eulau and Prewitt identified relationships between the goals, perceptions, and policy positions of city councilmen and public expenditures in their cities for planning and amenities. They found that the policy "images" of city councilmen were in accord with public spending patterns. They concluded:

> It has been the burden of our argument that the systematic study of public policy cannot be content with correlating indicators of environmental challenges or indicators of resource capability to policy outcomes. Rather it is our assumption that policy development is greatly influenced by the predictions, preferences, orientations, and expectations of policy makers—in short, by the political process itself.[26]

Yet it is important to point out that they did not systematically test to see if a councilman's attitudes affected the city policy *independently* of environmental variables. Apparently they were so convinced that the political ideologies of councilmen were important policy determinants that they felt that it was unnecessary to test this proposition. Of course, councilmen's ideologies were also associated with policy outcomes, but councilmen's ideologies were also associated with characteristics of city populations, and Eulau and Prewitt never attempted to sort out the independent effect of ideology on public policy from the effect of the urban environment.

But in Robert Eyestone's *The Threads of Public Policy,* councilmanic attitudes, images, and ideologies are systematically compared with certain environmental variables to ascertain their relative impact on public policy. Eyestone's work is a product of the City Council Research Project, and it is not especially designed as a test of what I believe to be the crucial issue—the *independent* effect of decision-makers' ideology on public policy. However, a careful examination of Eyestone's research does shed some light on this issue. Eyestone's definition of "policy" is very limited: (1) the percentage of total city spending for "Amenities," and (2) the percentage of total city spending for planning. Most of the book is devoted to showing relationships between characteristics of cities and the preferences, orientations, and images of councilmen toward zoning, development, and improvement of amenities. But at one point, Eyestone places aggregate measures of councilmanic views on "zoning problems," "development problems," and "amenities Improvements" in the same multiple regression problem on amenities expenditures *with* density, property value, city size, and growth rate.[27] The results seem to undermine much of the emphasis placed on decision-makers' attitudes: "For all groups [core cities, suburbs, and fringe cities], population density is overwhelmingly the best predictor." Indeed *density* alone explained 72 percent of variation among cities in amenities spending, with councilmanic attitudes contributing nothing of significance to the explanation of such spending. *Growth rate* explained 72 percent of the variation in core cities in planning expenditures. Only in suburbs and fringe cities were councilmanic attitudes independently related to planning expenditures. Eyestone's conclusions emphasize relationships between environment, councilmanic attitudes,

and public policy, which undoubtedly exist. But councilmanic attitudes seldom stray far from the constraints placed upon
them by the environment—population density, size, growth
rate, taxable property, etc. And there is not much evidence
presented to justify the conclusion that councilmanic attitudes *independently* affect public policy.

Directions in Urban Policy Research

What can we conclude from the research literature on the
determinants of municipal policy? Again it seems clear that
political scientists have placed too much emphasis on governmental structure and political environment in explaining
public policies of the nation's cities. As in the comparative
research on states and nations, the primary forces influencing
what city governments do arise from the socioeconomic environment—specifically the mix of resources and needs stem-
ming from the economic and social composition of city populations. Economists and sciologists have made great strides
in identifying the determinants of municipal taxing,
spending, and service levels. Political scientists, with their
professional interest in governmental structure and their
ideological commitment to reformism, have been able to
learn something about the socioeconomic determinants of the
success of reformism—that is, the likelihood of a city adopting manager government, nonpartisan elections, and at-large
constituencies. But only recently have we begun to sort out
the policy consequences of reform. Certainly the most interesting and challenging finding is that reform *reduces* the responsiveness of city governments to population needs.

It may turn out that future research on the policy consequences of reformism in American cities will demonstrate
that ethnic minorities, and especially blacks, are disadvantaged by reformism. We may learn that not only blacks and

other minorities are disadvantaged in representation by manager governments, nonpartisanships, and particularly at-large
elections, but also that reformed governments are less likely
to pursue policies which are responsive to the needs of these
groups. Thus, the traditional commitments of political scientists to municipal reform may be challenged by systematic
policy research.

4 METHODS IN POLICY ANALYSIS

Causal Thinking in Policy Research

One of the recognized shortcomings in public policy research is its failure to fully develop and test causal theories. This criticism generally applies to both policy *determination* research (where the antecedents to policy decisions are investigated), and to policy *impact* research (where the effects of policy decisions on society are under scrutiny). Most policy studies to date have relied primarily on associative reasoning and methodologies. Of course, exploring relationships between public policies and social, economic, and political characteristics of a society is a necessary step in the development of a policy science. And causal theories are often implicit in much of our policy research. But increasingly policy research must become concerned with the development of explicit causal models and the formal testing of causal linkages.

Most of the systematic, comparative research described earlier—research involving cities, states, and nations—described associations between environmental resources and demands, system characteristics, and public policies. But we must develop a better understanding of precisely *how* social economic or political forces go about shaping public policy, and precisely *how* public policies impact the social, economic, or political fashion. We must begin the difficult task of constructing causal models which portray developmental and sequential ideas about *how* socioeconomic and political forces and public policies interact. It may turn out to be the case, of course, that the necessary data for causal modeling is frequently unavailable, or that the available data violates assumptions of the statistical techniques employed in causal analysis, or even that the multiplicity of plausible causal models defies our patience in searching out the single best-fitting model. But causal thinking is still valuable if it forces us to think about the complexity of our task and the difficulty in actually understanding the inner workings and hidden mechanisms of social systems.

The Utility of Path Analysis

In my judgment, one of the most promising methods of clarifying our causal thinking about the causes and consequences of public policy is path analysis. Path analysis enables us (or compels us) to portray our ideas about the causes or consequences of public policy in diagrammatic fashion.

Path analysis, like regression analysis, provides an overall estimate of the explanatory value of a model. Path analysis also assists in identifying spurious relationships. More importantly, it permits the testing of both direct and indirect causal paths in the determination of a dependent variable. We can ascertain whether a determining variable acts on a dependent variable directly, or through mediating variables, or both; and we can compare the relative influence of direct and indirect causal paths.

Path analysis begins with the construction of a diagrammatic model in which *every* known determinant of a dependent variable is included in the system. Causal paths are represented by arrows which connect the dependent variable with every independent variable, both directly and indirectly through mediating variables which are themselves completely determined. The dependent variable is generally placed at the far right of the diagram; variables which are not dependent upon any other variables in the system are placed at the far left; and the variables which help to determine the dependent variable but which themselves are determined by other variables in the system are placed in between.

In a study of policy *determinants*, where we are analyzing the causes of public policy, the policy itself would be placed at the far right of the diagram and the direct and indirect causal paths are traced back through intermediate variables environmental conditions. In a study of policy *impacts*, where we are analyzing the consequences of public policy, the hypothesized impacts would be placed at the far right of the diagram and policy variables would be placed as intermediate variables, under the assumption that policies which impact some particular conditions are themselves shaped by other environmental conditions. This placement of policy variables in policy impact studies allows us to compare causal paths which flow *through* policy variables, with causal paths which proceed directly from environmental conditions to a presumed policy impact.

The placement of variables is a product of prior theoretical notions about the system. One must postulate time sequences, mechanisms of influence, and developmental processes in constructing a path analytic model. Knowledge of correlations is not enough. One must think about *how* variables might act on each other, and then construct a diagram which portrays these causal notions. The method of path analysis tests the notions which you have devised. But it cannot tell you what the true, real-world system of relations are.

Variables at the far left of the diagram which are not determined by other variables in the system may themselves be intercorrelated. These unanalyzed correlations are shown by *curved* arrows, which call attention to the distinction between a correlation and a path relating a dependent to a determining variable.

In order to provide for the *complete* determination of the dependent variable and the mediating variables, it is necessary to introduce an array of residual or error terms indicating unexplained variance. These residual or error terms are represented by arrows in the same fashion as direct and indirect causal paths.

Path coefficients are estimated from a series of simultaneous regression equations in which first the dependent variable is regressed against all other variables as independent variables, and the mediating variables are treated sequentially as dependent variables with socioeconomic variables as independent variables. The path coefficients are standardized b values, or "beta coefficients"; these are obtained by multiplying the b value by the standard deviation of the independent variable divided by the standard deviation of the dependent variable. The paths from the residual values are calculated as $1-R^2$—the square root of the unexplained variance in the multiple regression problems. The residual paths represent the effects of all unmeasured variables; but the adequacy of the model should not be judged by the size of the explained variance alone. It must also be judged by the relationships specified.

A causal path is eliminated from the hypothesized model if the *standard error* of any b value in any regression equation from a dependent variable to an independent variable is greater than the b value itself. The F statistic (analysis of variance) in such a case requires that the path be dropped from the causal model. The first series of simultaneous regression equations depicting the hypothesized model is only a first step: the primary purpose of these calculations is the elimination of paths which do not appear to make a significant contribution to variation in the dependent variable. A revised model with only influential paths represented is then calculated in a new series of regression equations. The revised model is simply the original model with paths erased where the corresponding b values turned out to be insignificant and negligible. In this new set of equations, the standardized b values, the "beta coefficients," become the *path coefficients.*

Assumptions of path analysis include the following: (1) that relationships are additive and linear, (2) that the residual "error" terms are uncorrelated, (3) that the causal paths involve no reciprocal causation, and (4) that the causal arrangement is appropriate. The first assumption is common in regression analysis; however, it should be noted that the presence of non-linear relationships may invalidate our conclusions. The second assumption is more troublesome. The only way of reducing the likelihood of outside error terms disturbing the equations is to bring into the model as explicit causal variables as many potentially disturbing influences as possible. The problem, of course, is that too many causal variables make the theoretical model unwieldy. Thus, we must trade off possibilities of reaching erroneous conclusions against the value of achieving a reasonable clear and simple model. The third assumption is that we know the directions in which the causal arrows point, and that no causal arrow points in two directions simultaneously. In other words, there must be no feedback loops occurring in the system. This assumption is also troublesome—particularly with regard to policy studies. One approach to the problem is to exercise care in time sequences between policy measures and environmental conditions. In a study of policy impacts, care must be exercised to insure that policies occur after their presumed antecedents.

Finally, the causal model itself must be a theoretically satisfying one. Needless to say, there will always be a number of plausible alternative models which will yield approximately the same predictions as the model under study. We can only proceed by *eliminating* hypothesized but inadequate models. It is ordinarily impossible to rule out all the logical alternative models. Thus, in a sense, one can never "establish" a particular causal model.

An Illustrative Model: Police Protection in American Cities*

Let us illustrate the wide uses of path analysis in a very simple exercise on the determinants of police protection in American cities. Variations in police protection are associated with a wide array of socioeconomic variables in American cities. Simple correlation coefficients based on 245 cities reveal that police manpower per 10,000 population is associated with size, income, race, and property-ownership, as well as crime rates and revenue levels.[3] But in order to explore causal relationships, some theoretical constructions are required.

Let us hypothesize that variations in police protection among cities may be either a product of different *demands*

---

*This illustration of the use of policy analysis was previously published by the author in the *Policy Studies Journal* Vol. 2 (Winter, 1973), and is used with the permission of the publisher.

for police protection, or different *resources* available to cities. Variables which may affect *demands* include the size, income, racial, and property-owning characteristics of a city's population. These socioeconomic characteristics may create demands directly: for example, a large, heavily non-white, non-property owning, low-income population may create a demand for increased police protection. Or these same socioeconomic characteristics may operate *indirectly* to create a demand for police proetection by affecting crime levels: A large, heavily non-white, non-property owning, low-income population may increase crime rates which *in turn* increase the demand for police protection. Of course, size, income, occupation, race and property-ownership also reflect a city's *resources* to provide any public service. These variables may affect police expenditures *indirectly* by affecting revenue levels which in turn enable a city to provide increased police protection.

The model in Figure 1 represents these initial notions about the possible direct and indirect determinant paths for urban police protection. (We do not believe that increases in crime rates cause increases in general revenue levels, or vice versa, even though these variables are related. Hence, this linkage is missing from our causal model.) Not all these paths will prove to have a determining impact on police protection. The broken line paths represent hypothesized relationships which did not produce path coefficients indicating a significant causal effect.

The series of simultaneous regression equations presented in Table 2 provide the calculations for determining the strength of causal paths in our hypothesized model. The regression coefficients (b values) and their standard errors are reported. Path coefficients are shown for only those causal paths which proved to be influential. In our model every path proved to be influential except two: from population size to crime rates and from income to police manpower.

The model succeeds in explaining 68 percent of the total variance in police expenditures among cities of 50,000 or more. As predicted, crime rates and revenue levels were influential determinants of police expenditures, suggesting the impact of both *demands* and *resources* on spending for police protection. But environmental variables—size, income, race and home ownership—also operated directly on police expenditures as well as *indirectly* through crime rates and revenue levels.

Race is the most influential environmental variable in the *demand* path to police protection. Race affects police expenditures *directly*: an increase in non-white populations percentage is associated with an increase in police manpower. And race also affects police expenditures *indirectly*: an increase in non-white population percentage is associated with an increase in crime rates which is in turn associated with an increase in police manpower.

Home ownership is the most influential environmental variable in the *resource* path to police expenditures. Home ownership affects police expenditures *directly*: an increase in home ownership is associated with a decrease in police protection. Home ownership also affects police protection *indirectly* by reducing municipal revenue levels which in turn affect police manpower. Home ownership is also influential in the demand path, although not *as* influential as race. Home ownership reduces the demand for police protection by reducing crime rates.

Size and *income* also contribute to the explanation of police protection, although their influence is not so great as race and home ownership. Size does not appear to affect crime rates (at least not variations in city size among cities over 50,000). But increases in size are modestly associated with increases in revenue levels and increases in police manpower.

Figure 1
Path Analysis: Police Manpower

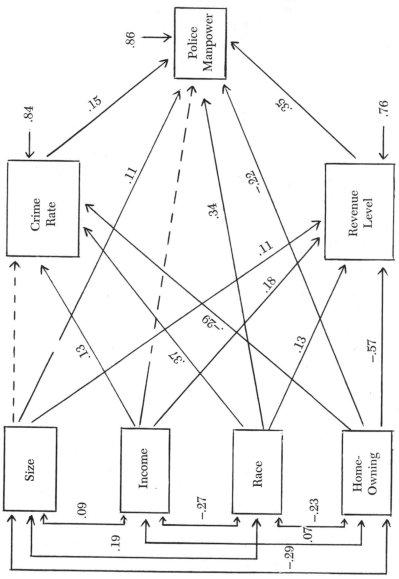

TABLE 5
REGRESSION EQUATIONS FOR PATH ANALYTIC MODELS FOR POLICE PROTECTION

	Population	Income	Race	Homeowning	Crime	Revenue	R^2
Police Manpower							
b. value	.16	.03	11.2	–10.6	10.3	.023	.68
s.e. of b	.05	.03	2.1	2.6	1.7	.004	.42
Path coef.	.11	*	.34	–.22	.15	.35	.30
Revenue							
b value	1.70	1.39	86.5	–420			
s.e. of b	.84	.40	36.0	38			
Path coef.	.11	.18	.13	–.57			
Crime Rate							
b value	.00	.002	.47	–.40			
s.e. of b	.00	.001	.07	.08			
Path coef.	*	.13	.37	–.29			

*Path eliminated, not significant.

Income is positively associated with crime rates, and revenue but there is no direct path from income to police protection, suggesting that income affects police protection only *indirectly* through increasing both crime and revenue levels.

Generally the *direct* path of the environmental variables are stronger that the *indirect* paths through either crime rates or revenue levels. This is largely a product of the fact that environmental variables explain less than half of the variation in crime rates and revenue levels. Since the environmental variables fail to account for half of the variation in these mediating factors, the influence of environmental forces *through* these factors is weakened. Nonetheless, both the demand (crime rate) path and resource (revenue level) path are confirmed by the coefficients. The path of property ownership through revenue levels to police expenditures is the strongest of the indirect paths.

Perhaps the most noteworthy finding of this brief analytic exercise is that police manpower increases as a *direct* result of non-white populations increase, regardless of the effect of these increases on the crime rate! There is no question that black population increases affect crime rates; this finding has been reported frequently.[4] But path analysis suggests that black population increases produce increase police expenditures and police manpower *beyond* the increases coming about through increased crime rates. It is doubtful that blacks themselves are demanding these increases in police manpower. (Correlations among aggregate populations do not permit inferences about individual behavior.) We are tempted to speculate that *white* populations demand increased police protection when black population percentages increase—that *they demand more police protection than required to cope with the increased crime rates.*

An Illustrative Model: Welfare Spending in the States

The path analytic technique has been employed to shed more light on the effect of political competition and participation on welfare spending in the American states. As we observed in Chapter 2, pluralist ideology had posited an important role for competition and participation in determining levels of asistance for "have nots"—including expenditures per recipient in AFDC programs. However, a number of empirical studies had suggested that economic development —income, urbanization, industrialization—had a more important impact on public policy, including welfare policy, than participation or competition. Political scientist Gary Tompkins designed a model to clarify these relationships: a model in which industrialization was perceived as antecedent to participation and competition; and all of these variables were perceived as factors influencing levels of aid to dependent children in the states.

This model succeeds in explaining 69 percent of the variation among the states in levels of aid to dependent children. But the interesting aspect of the causal model (See Figure 4-2) and the path analysis employed to test it, is the sorting out of significant causal sequences. Figure 4-2 presents only those linkages for which significant path coefficients were obtained. Note that ethnicity is related to income (immigrants came to the wealthier states); higher incomes produce party competition which in turn produces voter participation; party competition has some direct effect on welfare benefits; but it is *ethnicity* which is most closely related to welfare benefits. This model shows *no* direct path between income and welfare benefits when ethnicity is part of the model. This finding contrasts with earlier research which indicated a direct linkage between income and welfare benefits; the difference in outcomes appears to be a result of

Figure 2

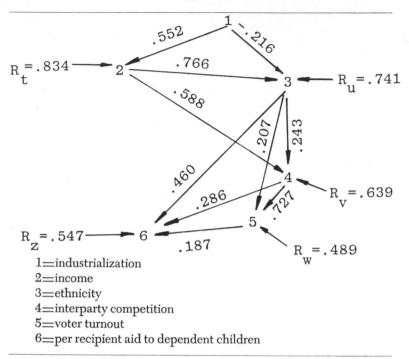

1=industrialization
2=income
3=ethnicity
4=interparty competition
5=voter turnout
6=per recipient aid to dependent children

Source: Gary Tompkins, "A Causal Model of State Welfare Expenditures," *Journal of Politics* Vol. 37 (May, 1975), 392–416.

adding ethnicity to the model. In short, Tompkins uses this path analytic model to suggest that *neither* income *nor* competition-participation are as important in determining welfare benefits as ethnicity.

An Illustrative Model: Social Welfare Spending Among Nations

Another illustration of the utliity of path analysis can be found in Harold Wilensky's cross-national investigation of the determinants of welfare state spending.[5] Wilensky's dependent variable was "social security effort" as measured by the percentage of a nation's GNP devoted to social security expenditures. His independent variables were:

—Age of the social security system
    (log sum of years operation of five social security programs)
—Age of the population
    (percentage of the population of age 65 years and over)
—Totalitarian state
    (presence or absence of totalitarian government)
—Liberal Democratic State
    (presence or absence of liberal democratic state)
—Economic Level
    (GNP per capita)

His units of analysis were 60 nations.

Wilensky's initial regression analysis indicated that these independent variables succeeded in explaining 83 percent of the variance among nations in social security effort. Path analysis was employed to unscramble the significant causal sequences among these variables and to construct a model that made theoretical sense. Wilensky's model is reproduced as Figure 3. Wilensky chose to include arrows only where significant paths were discovered. We can assume that all other possible paths in the model in Figure 3 "washed out," that is, failed to produce significant path coefficients.

What does Wilensky's path analytic model suggest? Although economic level and social security effect are strongly correlated (the simple correlation coefficient, now shown, is .67), the path diagram shows that this relationship is *mediated* first by the proportion of aged population, and second through both aged population and age of social security system. There is no direct path from economic level to social security effort only *through* its intervening effect on in-

Figure 3

Causal Model of Social Security
Spending: 60 Countries

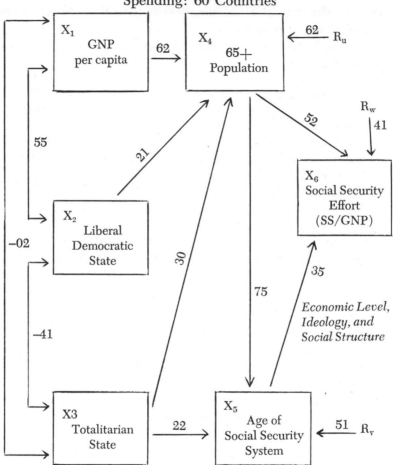

Solid lines indicate relationships with $p < .05$; nonsignificant paths have
been omitted.

Source: Harold Wilensky *The Welfare State and Equality* (Berkeley
University of California Press, 1975), p. 25.

creasing the proportion of aged in the population, and initiating a social security system at an earlier date. Linkages between democratic and totalitarian political systems and these mediating variables are weaker than the linkage with economic development.

The model permits Wilensky to theorize about the *causes* of social security spending:

> For this sixty-country sample, the primacy of economic level and its demographic and bureaucratic correlates is support for a convergence hypothesis; economic growth makes countries with contrasting cultural and political traditions more alike in their strategy for constructing the floor below which no one sinks. Further evidence of convergence of rich countries is the finding that authoritarian polities have no significant effects net of economic level, while the other two types of political systems, liberal democracy and totalitarianism, have only a small independent influence on social security effort. And insofar as they count, the two systems work in the same direction—increased welfare effort. Incidentally, the path diagram (fig. 1) shows that the small influence of the two political types is entirely indirect; liberal democracy makes its contribution through age of population and age of system and through its correlation with GNP; totalitarianism makes its contribution through age of population and age of system.[5]

Path Analysis in Policy Research

As policy research becomes increasingly theory-oriented, it will require increasingly complex causal models and appropriate methodologies for testing these models. Our brief illustrations suggest the way in which path analysis can be employed to better understand policy *determination*. But path analysis also provides a useful technique in studies of policy impact. Policy measures can be portrayed as mediating variables in causal models, and path coefficients can allow us to compare the direct effects of environmental variables on societal changes, with the indirect effects flowing through policy measures. In general, path analysis is a more powerful tool in causal modeling than earlier Simon-Blalock techniques. Of course, no methodology substitutes for thinking about what is happening in the real world.

5 THE CHALLENGE OF A POLICY SCIENCE

Assessing the Impact of Public Policy

Policy "impacts" are changes in the society which are brought about as a result of some government activity. Policy impacts are the *consequences* of government activity. These are not merely measures of government activity—how much money is spent, how much public effort is being made, in a particular area—but rather measures of changes in the environment or the political system caused by government actions. Research on the impact of public policy requires social scientists to treat policy as the *independent* variable and societal conditions as *dependent* variables.

The study of policy impacts (or "policy evaluation" as it is frequently called in public administration) is increasingly being recognized as an important responsibility of political scientists, and social scientists generally. No longer do we *assume* that once we pass a law, establish a bureaucracy, and spend money, that the purpose of these acts will be achieved and the results will be what we expected them to be. The national experiences with the "war on poverty," public housing,

95

urban renewal, public assistance, and many other public programs indicate the need for careful appraisals of the real impact of public policy. Decision-makers, themselves, are increasingly concerned with the costs and effectiveness of many public service and social action programs. Increasingly they are turning to policy analysts to ask questions about the impact of ongoing or proposed programs—what, if anything, do they accomplish? why do we need them? what do they cost? who do they help? what are their spillover effects on others? who bears the burden of their costs? what are their long-range as well as short run consequences? are there more effective ways of producing similar results? how do we choose wisely between programs with different social goals? Decison-makers do not always get good answers to these questions yet, for reasons we will explain later. But the need for systematic research on policy impacts is widely recognized.

In the interesting book *Systematic Thinking for Social Action* by Alice Rivlin of the Brookings Institution, a book based in part on her experience as Assistant Secretary for Planning and Evaluation for HEW, Ms. Rivlin summarizes the current "state of the art" in policy impact research:

1. Considerable progress has been made in identifying and measuring social problems in our society. Much more is known about who is poor or sick or badly educated, and this knowledge itself has helped clarify policy choices.

2. Systematic analysis has improved our knowledge of the distribution of the initial costs and benefits of social action programs. Much more is known about who wins and who loses.

3. Little progress has been made in comparing the benefits of different social action problems. It is not possible, for example, to say whether it would do society more good to cure cancer or to teach poor children to read.

4. Little in known about how to produce more effective

health, education, and other social services. Unfortunately, moreover, neither social service systems nor federal programs are organized to find out.

Let us explore some of the obstacles to systematic policy research—obstacles confronting both government administrators and social scientists.

Why Governmental Agencies Do Poor Policy Research

Attempts at policy evaluation are now common in federal programs. Frequently administrative analysts report on the conditions of target groups before and after their participation in a new program, and some effort is made to attribute observed changes to the new program itself. But governmental agencies are ill-suited for studying the impact of their own activities. Let us suggest some reasons for this:

1. Many programs and policies have primarily symbolic value. They do not actually change the conditions of target groups but merely make these groups feel that government "cares." A government agency does not welcome a study which reveals that its efforts have no tangible effects; such a revelation itself might reduce the symbolic value of the program by informing target groups of its uselessness.

2. Government agencies have a strong vested interest in "proving" that their programs have a positive impact. Administrators frequently view attempts to evaluate the impact of their progarms as attempts to limit or destroy their programs, or to question the competence of the administrators.

3. Government agencies usually have a heavy investment —organizational, financial, physical, psychological—in current programs and policies. They are predisposed against finding that these policies do not work.

4. Any serious study of policy impact undertaken by a government agency would involve some interference with

ongoing program activities. The press of day-to-day business generally takes priority over study and evaluation in a governmental agency. More important, the conduct of an experiment may necessitate depriving individuals or groups (control groups) of services to which they are entitled under law; this may be difficult, if not impossible, to do.

5. Program evaluation requires funds, facilities, time, and personnel which government agencies do not like to sacrifice from ongoing programs. Policy impact studies, like any research, cost money. They cannot be done well as extracurricular or part-time activities. Devoting resources to study may mean a sacrifice in program resources that administrators are unwilling to make.

6. There is generally wide disagreement about what the purposes of a government program really are. Is the object to serve as many people as possible? Or to bring about a great deal of change in the lives of fewer people? Or merely to make people happy—particularly Congressmen and other elected officials? Government administrators themselves frequently disagree about the purposes of the program.

Social Science Research and Policy Evaluation: The Busing Controversy

But social scientists also confront a myriad of problems in conducting systematic research on controversial social problems. Let me illustrate some of these problems with reference to social science research on busing and equality of educational opportunity.

One of the more interesting examples of policy-relevant research by social scientists in recent years in the influential report on American education by James S. Coleman, "Equality of Educational Opportunity," frequently referred to as the "Coleman Report."[1] While the Coleman Report is not without its critics, it is nonetheless the most comprehensive analysis of the American public school system ever made. The Coleman Report was eighteen months in the making; it cost $2 million to produce; and it included data on 600,000 children, 60,000 teachers, and 4,000 schools.

The result of Coleman's study undermined much of the conventional wisdom about the impact of public educational policies on student learning and achievement. Prior to the study, most of the U. S. generally assumed that factors such as the number of pupils in the classroom, the amount of money spent on each pupil, library and laboratory facilities, teachers' salaries, the quality of the curriculum and other characteristics of the school, affected the quality of education and educational opportunity. But systematic analysis revealed that these factors had *no* significant effect on student learning or achievement. "Differences in school facilities and curriculum . . . are so little related to differences in achievement levels of students that, with few exceptions, their effects fail to appear even in a survey of this magnitude." Moreover, learning was found to be unaffected by the presence or absence of a "track system," ability grouping, guidance counseling, or other standard educational programs. Even the size of the class was found to be unrelated to learning, although educationalists had asserted the importance of this factor for decades. Finally, the Coleman study reported that the quality of teaching was not a very significant factor in student achievement compared to family and peer group influences.

The only factors that were found to affect a student's learning to any significant degree were his family background and the family background of his fellow students. Family background affected the child's verbal abilities and attitudes toward education, and these factors correlated very closely with scholastic achievement. Of secondary but consi-

derable significance were the verbal abilities and attitudes toward education of the child's classmates. Peer-group influence had its greatest impact on children from lower-class
families. Teaching excellence mattered very little to children
from upper and middle-class backgrounds; they learned well
despite mediocre or poor teaching. Children from lower-class
families were slightly more affected by teacher quality.

Reanalyzing Coleman's data for the U. S. Civil Rights
Commission, Thomas F. Pettigrew and others found that
black students attending predominantly black schools had
lower achievement scores and lower levels of aspiration than
black students with comparable family backgrounds who attended predominantly white schools.[2] When black students
attending predominantly white schools were compared with
black students attending predominantly black schools, the
average difference in levels of achievement amounted to
more than two grade levels.

The Coleman Report made no policy recommendations.
But, like a great deal of policy research, policy recommendations can easily be implied from its conclusions. First of all, if
the Coleman Report is correct, it seems pointless to simply
pour more money into the present system of public education—raising per pupil expenditures, increasing teachers' salaries, lowering the number of pupils per classroom, providing
better libraries and laboratories, adding educational frills, or
adopting any specific curricula innovations. These policies
were found to have no significant impact on learning.

Thus, the Coleman Report implies that compensatory programs have little educational value. They may have symbolic
value indicating society's concern for equal educational opportunity; or political value for officeholders who seek to
establish an image of concern for the underprivileged, but
they have little impact on the achievement or aspiration
levels of children.

The U. S. Commission on Civil Rights used the Coleman Report to buttress its policy proposals to end racial imbalance in public schools in both the North and the South. Inasmuch as money, facilities, and compensatory programs have little effect on a student learning, and inasmuch as the socioeconomic background of the student's classmates does affect his learning, it seemed reasonable to argue that the assignment of lower-class black students to predominantly middle-class white schools would be the only way to improve educational opportunities for ghetto children. Hence, the Commission called for an end to neighborhood schools and the *busing* of black and white children to racially balanced schools.

Since its publication, the Coleman Report has been frequently cited by proponents of "busing"—those urging deliberate government action to achieve racial balance in public schools. Courts and school officials in northern and southern cities have cited the Coleman Report as evidence that racial imbalance denies equality of educational opportunity to black children, and as evidence that deliberate racial balancing in the schools, or "busing," is required to achieve equal protection of laws.

But in 1972, Harvard sociologist David Armor shocked the academic world with a careful review of the available evidence of the effect of busing on the achievement levels of black students.[3] His conclusions: black students bussed out of their neighborhood to predominantly white schools do not improve their performance relative to white students, even after three or four years of integrated education. His interpretation of the impact of busing on the achievement levels of black students indicated that black students were not being helped "in any significant way" by busing, and he even urged consideration of the question of whether psychological harm was being done to black students by placing them in a situation where the achievement gap was so great.

Note that Armor was not contradicting the Coleman Report. Coleman was observing black children who were attending predominantly white schools not as a result of deliberate government action, but rather within the previously existing pattern of "neighborhood schools." In contrast, Armor was observing black children who had been deliberately reassigned to integrated schools by government action.

The policy implications of Armor's work appear to support opponents of government mandated racial balancing. Other social scientists have disputed Armor's review of the relevant research findings, including Thomas F. Pettigrew, who originally used the Coleman data in support of busing.[4] But Armor argues that social science findings cannot be used only when they fit the political beliefs of social scientists, and ignored when their policy implications are painful.[5]

Still another reaction to the Coleman Report is found in the work of Harvard educationalist Christopher Jencks, entitled *Inequlaity*.[6] Jencks reanalyzed Coleman's data and conducted additional research on the impact of schooling on economic success He found that school quality has little effect on an individual's subsequent success in earning income. He concluded, therefore, that no amount of educational reform would ever bring about economic equality. Jencks assumed that *absolute equality* of income is the goal of society, not merely *equality of opportunity* to achieve economic success. Since the schools cannot insure that everyone ends up with the same income, Jencks concludes that nothing short of a radical redistribution of income (steeply progressive taxes and laws preventing individuals from earning more than others) will bring about true equality in America. Attempts to improve the educational system are a waste of time and effort. Thus, the Coleman findings have been used to buttress *radical* arguments about the ineffectiveness of *liberal* reforms.

The point of this brief discussion of the Coleman Report is

that policy analysis sometimes produces unexpected and even embarrassing findings, that public policies do not always "work" as intended, and that different political interests will interpret the findings of policy research differently —accepting, rejecting, or using these findings as it fits their own purposes.

Obstacles to the Development of a Policy Science

Let us try to summarize some of the problems that political scientists must expect to confront as they undertake to construct policy science.

1. First of all, political science must acquire a scientific mood of skepticism in assessing the consequences of public policies. Support for liberal reform must be tempered by careful and systematic assessment of the actual consequences of liberal and reformist programs and policies. The political values of most social scientists predispose them to believe that liberal reforms will produce positive results. When reforms appear to do so, the research results are immediately accepted and published; but when results are unsupportive or negative, social scientists are inclined to go back and recode their data, or redesign their research, or reevaluate their results, because they believe a "mistake" must have been made. Moreover, "successful" research—where the results demonstrate clear and positive policy impact—receives more acclaim and produces greater opportunities for advancement for social scientists, than "unsuccessful" research—where the results fail to show any clear or positive impact of a particular public policy. But negative findings —proof of the null hypothesis—are just as important in the development of a policy science as positive findings. My point is that the systematic policy science must treat liberal and reformist notions as hypotheses to be tested, not as a priori

assumptions. My plea is for a scientific posture in political science which designs policy research in such a way so as to control, insofar as possible, our predispositions, values, and biases.

2. A second set of obstacles in the development of a policy science centers about inherent limitations in the design of policy research. First, consider the problems in *experimental* research designs: Do governmental researchers have the right to withhold public services from some individuals simply to provide a control group for experimentation? What are we to say to control groups who are chosen to be similar to experimental groups but denied benefits in order to serve as a basis for comparison? Setting aside the legal and moral issues, it will be politically difficult to provide services for some people and not to others. Perhaps only the fact that relatively few Americans knew about the New Jersey income maintenance experiment kept it from becoming a controversial topic. Another problem is that people behave differently when they know they are being watched. Students for example generally perform at a higher level when something —anything—new and different is introduced into the classroom routine. This "Hawthorne effect" may cause a new program or reform to appear more successful than the old, but it is the newness itself which produces improvement rather than the program or the reform. Another problem in policy experimentation is that results obtained with small-scale experiments may differ substantially from what would occur if a large scale, nation-wide program were adopted. In the New Jersey experiments, if only one family receives income maintenance payments in a neighborhood, its members may continue to behave as their neighbors do. But if everyone in the nation is guaranteed a minimum income, community standards may change and affect the behavior of all recipient families.

But the problems are equally intractable in non-experimental research designs. Policy analysts must attempt to determine the impact of public policies by studying conditions of individuals or groups who have enjoyed the benefits of a policy and compare them with those who have not. But it is extraordinarily difficult to control all of the factors which go into these real-world "natural" experiments. In time-series studies, it is difficult to sort out the changes which come about because of the introduction of a particular program or policy from changes which are occurring in society anyhow. In cross-sectional studies, it is difficult to attribute differences in schools, communities, states, or nations to the effects of particular policies or programs,, when there are so many other social, economic, or cultural forces at work shaping societies.

3. Perhaps an even more serious obstacle is the "subjectivity" of policy research. Policy analysts cannot offer "solutions" to problems when there is not any general agreement on what the problems are. Policy research brings social scientists directly into the political process. Even the selection of a topic for research—the statement of a problem to be solved—is affected by one's values of what is "important" in society and worthy of attention. Policy research, therefore, cannot be "value free." Recently James Q. Wilson formulated two general laws to cover all cases of social science research on policy impact:

Wilson's First Law: All policy interventions in social problems produce the intended effect—*if* the research is carried out by those implementing the policy or their friends.

Wilson's Second Law: No policy intervention in social problems produces the intended effect—*if* the research is carried out by independent third parties, especially those skeptical of the policy. (Interestingly, Wilson was commenting

on the Armor study and Armor's critics, particularly Thomas
F. Pettigrew.)

Wilson denies that his laws are cynical. Instead he reasons that:

> Studies that conform to the First Law will accept an
> agency's own data about what it is doing and with what
> effect; adopt a time frame (long or short) that maximizes
> the probability of observing the desired effect; and mini-
> mize the search for other variables that might account for
> the effect observed. Studies that conform to the Second Law
> will gather data independently of the agency; adopt a short
> time frame that either minimizes the chance for the desired
> effect to appear or, if it does appear, permits one to argue
> that the results are "temporary" and probably due to the
> operation of the "Hawthorne Effect" (i.e., the reaction of
> the subjects to the fact that they are part of an experiment);
> and maximize the search for other variables that might
> explain the effects observed.[7]

4. Another obstacle to the development of a policy science within the discipline of political science is the narrow
and restricted definition of our discipline which limits the
attention of political scientists to governmental institutions
and political processes. The professional preoccupation of
political scientists has always been with the characteristics
of political systems—party competition, interest group activity, malapportionment, the powers of president, congress,
and courts, voting behavior, and so forth. But the development of a policy science will require political scientists to
become more and more interdisciplinary in their interests and
in their training. Political scientists must be prepared to examine the consequences of public policies in areas as diverse
as education, welfare, health, housing, the environment, national defense, the economy, and foreign affairs. Clearly,

then, for political science to become a policy science, it must become more interdisciplinary in character—incorporating concepts, methods, and measurements drawn from a wide variety of disciplines, not only in the social sciences, but also in the physical and biological sciences.

5. Perhaps the most serious reservation about the development of a policy science is the fact that societal problems are so complex that social scientists may be unable to make accurate predictions about the impact of proposed policies. In other words, social scientists simply may not know enough about individual and group behavior to be able to give reliable advice to policy-makers. Policy makers turn to social scientists for "solutions" to societal problems—government interventions that will produce intended changes in society. But social scientists simply do not have many interventionalist solutions. Social science research which reveals complex causal factors in a societal problem, and which fails to provide decision-makers with a convenient handle to cope with the problem, can only frustrate decision-makers. They are not as interested in explanations of societal problems as they are in ways to manipulate societal conditions through government action. But most of society's problems are shaped by so many variables that a simple remedy for them —a governmental program which "solves" the problem—is rarely possible. The fact that social scientists give so many contradictory policy recommendations is an indication of the absence of reliable scientific knowledge about social problems.

Despite these obstacles to the development of a policy science, it seems safe to say that reason, knowledge, and analysis are still appropriate tools in the consideration of policy questions. Policy analysis may not provide solutions to America's problems. But we do not need to rely exclusively on "rules of thumb" or "muddling through" or "rap sessions" or "sounding off" in approaching policy questions. We can commit ourselves to the task of systematically describing and explaining the causes and consequences of public policy not only to advance scientific understanding, but also to improve the quality of public policy.

NOTES

Notes to Chapter 1

[1] Yehezkel Dror, "The Challenge of Policy Sciences," *Policy Studies Journal* Vol. 1 (Autumn, 1972), p. 4.

[2] The following account of the Head Start evaluation study relies mainly on Walter Williams and John W. Evans, "The Politics of Evaluation: The Case of Head Start," Annals of the American Academy of Social and Political Science (September, 1969), 118-132.

[3] Westinghouse Learning Corporation – Ohio University, *The Impact of Head Start: An Evaluation of the Effects of Head on Children's Cognitive and Affective Development* (Washington: Office of Economic Opportunity, 1969).

[4] See James E. Anderson, *Public Policy-Making* (New York: Paeger, 1975), p. 150.

[5] However, according to Williams and Evans: "In terms of its methodological and conceptual base, the study is a *relatively* good one. This in no way denies that many of the criticisms of the study are valid. However, for the most part they are the kinds of criticisms that can be made of most pieces of social science research conducted outside of the laboratory, in a real world setting, with all of the logistical and measurement problems that such studies entail." *Op. Cit.*, p. 129.

[6] See Harold M. Watts, "Graduated Work Incentives: An Experiment in Negative Taxation," *American Economic Review* Vol. 59 (May, 1969), 463-472.

[7] U.S. Office of Economic Opportunity, "Preliminary Results of the New Jersey Graduated Work Incentive Experiment," Feb-

ruary 18, 1970. Also Cited by Alice M. Rivlin, *Systematic Thinking for Social Action* (Washington: Brookings Institution, 1971).

[8] Edward Suchman, *Evaluative Research* (New York: Russell Sage Foundation, 1967).

Notes to Chapter 2

[1] For an introduction to the literature in political science dealing with policy analysis, see Thomas R. Dye, *Understanding Public Policy* (Englewood Cliffs: Prentice Hall, 1972); Ira Sharkansky (ed.), *Policy Analysis in Political Science* (Chicago: Markham, 1970).

[2] V. O. Key, Jr., *American State Politics* (New York: Knopf, 1956); Duane Lockard, *The Politics of State and Local Government* (New York: Macmillan, 1963); John H. Fenton, *People and Parties in Politics* (Flenview: Scott, Foresman, 1966).

[3] Solomon Fabricant, *The Trend of Government Activity in the United States Since 1900* (New York: National Bureau of Economic Research, 1950).

[4] Glenn W. Fisher, "Interstate Variation in State and Local Government Expenditures," *National Tax Journal* Vol. 17 (March, 1964), pp. 57-74.

[5] Seymour Sachs and Robert Harris, "The Determinants of State and Local Government Expenditures and Intergovernmental Flow of Funds," *National Tax Journal* Vol. 17 (March, 1974), pp. 78-85.

[6] Austin Ranney and Wilmoore Kendall, "The American Party System," *American Political Science Review* Vol. 48 (March, 1954), pp. 477-485; V. O. Key, Jr., *American State Politics* (New York: Knopf, 1956), p. 99; Joseph A. Schlesinger, "A Two-Dimensional Party Competition," *American Political Science Review,* Vol. 49 (1955), pp. 1120-28; Robert T. Golembiewski, "A Taxanomic Approach to State Political Party Strength," *Western Political Quarterly,* Vol. 11 (1958), pp. 419-513.

[7] Richard E. Dawson and James A. Robinson, "Inter-Party Competition, Economic Variables, and Welfare Policies in the American States," *Journal of Politics,* Vol. 25 (May, 1963), pp. 265-89.

[8] Thomas R. Dye, *Politics, Economics, and the Public* (Chicago: Rand McNally, 1966).

[9] The early works include Richard E. Dawson and James A. Robinson, "Interparty Competition, Economic Variables and Welfare Politics in the American States," *Journal of Politics*, 25 (May, 1963), pp. 265-289, Richard Hofferbert, "The Relation between Public Policy and Some Structural and Environmental Variables in the American States," *American Political Science Review*, 60 (March, 1966), pp. 73-82; Thomas R. Dye, "Malapportionment and Public Policy in the States," *Journal of Politics*, 27 (February, 1965), pp. 586-601, Herbert Jacob, "The Consequences of Malapportionment: A Note of Caution," *Social Forces*, 48 (1964), p. 261.

[10] Ira Sharkansky and Richard Hofferbert, "Dimensions of State Politics, Economics and Public Policy," *American Political Science Review*, 63 (September, 1969), pp. 867-879, and Thomas R. Dye, "Income Equality and American State Politics," *American Political Science Review*, Vol. 63 (March, 1969), pp. 157-162.

[11] Charles F. Cnudde and Donald J. McCrone, "Party Competition and Welfare Policies in the American States," *American Political Science Review*, Vol. 63 (September 1969), pp. 858-866.

[12] Ira Sharkansky, "Agency Requests Gubernatorial Support and Budget in State Legislatures," *American Political Science Review*, 62 (December, 1968), pp. 1220-1231, and Thomas R. Dye, "Executive Power and Public Policy in the States," *Western Political Quarterly*, 22 (December, 1969)), pp. 926-939.

[13] Bryan R. Fry and Richard Winters, "The Politics of Redistribution," *American Political Science Review*, 64 (June, 1970), Jack Walker, "The Diffusion of Innovations among the American States," *American Political Science Review*, 63 (September, 1969), pp. 867-879, and Thomas R. Dye, "Inequality and Civil Rights Policy in the States," *Journal of Politics*, 31 (November, 1969), pp. 1080-1097.

[14] Richard Hofferbert, "Ecological Development and Policy Change," *Midwest Journal of Political Science*, 10 (November, 1966), pp. 464-483.

[15] Sharkansky and Hofferbert, "Dimensions of State Politics,

Economics, and Public Policy," and Cnudde and Donald J. McCrone, "Party Competition and Welfare Policies in the American States."

[16] Ira Sharkansky, "Environment, Policy, Output and Input: Problems of Theory and Method in the Analysis of Public Policy," in Ira Sharkansky (ed.), *Policy Analysis in Political Science* (Chicago: Markham, 1970).

[17] James C. Strouse and J. Oliver Williams, "A Non-Addictive Model for State Policy Research," *Journal of Politics* Vol. 34 (May, 1972), pp. 648-657.

[18] Of course, not all of this literature has been good. See, for example, John Crittenden, "Dimensions of Modernization in the American States," *American Political Science Review*, 61 (December, 1967), pp. 982-1002, Alan G. Pulsipher and James L. Weatherby, "Malapportionment, Party Competition, and the Functional Distribution of Government Expenditures," *American Political Science Review*, 62 (December, 1968), pp. 1207-1220.

[19] Guenther F. Schaefer and Stuart Rakoff, "Politics, Policy, and Political Science," *Politics and Society*, Vol. 1 (November, 1970), p. 52.

[20] Richard Hofferbert, "Socioeconomic Dimensions of the American States, 1890-1960," *Midwest Journal of Political Science* Vol. 2 (August, 1968), pp. 401-418, Richard Hofferbert, "Ecological Development and Policy Change," *Midwest Journal of Political Science* Vol. 10 (November, 1966), pp. 464-483.

[21] Charles F. Cnudde and Donald J. McCrone, *op. cit.*; Ira Sharkansky and Richard Hofferbert, *op. cit.*

[22] Gary L. Tompkins, "A Causal Model of State Welfare Expenditures," *Journal of Politics*, Vol. 37 (May, 1975), 392-416.

[23] See Thomas R. Dye, *Understanding Public Policy* (Englewood Cliffs: Prentice Hall, 1972), pp. 251-254.

[24] Bryan R. Fry and Richard Winters, "The Politics of Redistribution," *American Political Science Review,* Vol. 64 (June, 1970), pp. 508-522.

[25] John L. Sullivan, "A Note on Redistributive Politics," *American Political Science Review*, Vol. 66 (December, 1972), pp. 1301-1305.

[26] Ira Sharkansky, "The Political Scientist and Policy Analysis," *Policy Analysis in Political Science, op. cit.,* p. 8; and Ira Sharkansky, "Dimensions of State Policy," in Herbert Jacob and Kenneth Vines (eds.), *Politics in the American States,* 2nd ed., (Boston: Little, Brown, 1971), p. 320.

[27] Seymour Sachs and Robert Harris, "The Determinants of State and Local Government Expenditures and Intergovernmental Flow of Funds," *National Tax Journal,* Vol. 17 (March, 1964), 75-85; Jack W. Osman, "On the Use of Aid as an Expenditure Determinant," *National Tax Journal,* Vol. 21 (December, 1968), 437-447.

[28] Thomas R. Dye, *Understanding Public Policy,* 2nd ed. (Englewood Cliffs: Prentice Hall, 1974), pp. 284-288.

[29] Roy W. Bahl and Robert J. Saunders, "Determinants of Changes in State and Local Government Expenditures," *National Tax Journal* Vol. 18 (March, 1965), 50-57.

[30] James C. Strouse and Philipp Jones, "Federal Aid: The Forgotten Variable in State Policy Research," *Journal of Politics,* Vol. 36 (February, 1964), 200-207.

[31] Douglas D. Rose, "National and Local Forces in State Politics," *American Political Science Review,* Vol. 67 (December, 1973), 1162-1173; and Thomas R. Dye, "Communication," *American Political Science Review,* Vol. 68 (December, 1974), 1264-1265.

[32] Charles Lindbloom, "The Science of Muddling Through," *Public Administration Review,* 19, (Spring, 1959), pp. 79-88, and *The Intelligence of Democracy* (New York: Free Press, 1966).

[33] Charles Lindbloom, *Public Administration Review, op. cit.,* Aaron Wildavsky, *Politics of the Budgetary Process* (Boston: Little, Brown, 1964), and Sharkansky, *Spending in the American States.*

[34] Ira Sharkansky, *Spending in the American States,* and "Economic and Political Correlates of State Government Expenditures," *Midwest Journal of Political Science,* 11 (May, 1967), pp. 173-192.

[35] Ira Sharkansky, "Some More Thoughts About the Determi-

nants of Government Expenditures," *National Tax Journal*, (June, 1967), p. 179.

[56] Robert L. Harlow, "Sharkansky on State Expenditures: A Comment," *National Tax Journal*, 21 (June, 1968), pp. 215-216.

[57] Jack L. Walker, "The Diffusion of Innovations Among the American States," *American Political Science Review*, Vol. 63 (September, 1969), 880-899.

[85] Virginia Grey, "Innovation in the States," *American Political Science Review*, Vol. 67 (December, 1973), 1174-1185.

[89] Thomas R. Dye, *Understanding Public Policy*, 2nd Ed. (Englewood Cliffs: Prentice Hall, 1975), 321-324.

[40] Phillips Cutright, "Political Structure, Economic Development, and National Social Security Programs," *American Journal of Sociology*, Vol. 70 (March, 1965), pp. 537-550.

[41] *Ibid.*, p. 550.

[42] Frederick L. Pryor, *Public Expenditures in Communist and Capitalistic Nations* (Homewood: Richard D. Irvin, 1968).

[43] *Ibid.*, pp. 310-311.

[44] Harold L. Wilensky, *The Welfare State and Equality* (Berkeley: University of California Press, 1975).

[45] Arnold J. Heidenheimer, "The Politics of Public Education, Health, and Welfare in the USA and Western Europe," *British Journal of Political Science*, Vol. 3 (1973), pp. 315-340.

[56] Larry L. Wade, *The Elements of Public Policy* (Columbus: Charles E. Merrill, 1972), pp. 33-41.

Notes to Chapter 3

[1] John H. Kessel, "Governmental Structure and Political Enviroment," *American Political Science Review* (September, 1962), pp. 615-620; Edgar L. Sherbenou, "Class, Participation, and the Council-Manager Plan," *Public Administration Review* (Summer, 1961), pp. 131-135; Phillips Cutright, "Nonpartisan Election Systems in American Cities," *Comparative Studies in Society and History* (January, 1963), pp. 212-226; Robert R. Alford and Harry M. Scoble, "Political and Socio-economic Characteristics of Amer-

ican Cities," *Municipal Yearbook* (Chicago: International City Managers Association, 1965), pp. 82-97.

[2] Brett W. Hawkins, *Politics and Urban Policy* (Columbus: Bobbs-Merrill, 1971), p. 55.

[3] Robert R. Alford and Harry M. Scoble, *op. cit.*, p. 83.

[4] Harvey Brazer, *City Expenditures in the United States* (New York: National Bureau of Economic Research, 1959).

[5] For a summary and analysis of this research, see John C. Weicher, "Determinants of Central City Expenditures: Some Overlooked Factors and Problems," *National Tax Journal*, Vol. 23 (December, 1970), pp. 379-396.

[6] Woo Sik Kee, "Central City Expenditures and Metropolitan Areas," *National Tax Journal*, Vol. 18 (December, 1965), pp. 337-353.

[7] Jack W. Osman, "The Dual Impact of Federal Aid on State and Local Government Expenditures," *National Tax Journal*, Vol. 19 (December, 1966), pp. 362-372; David L. Smith, "The Response of State and Local Governments to Federal Grants," *National Tax Journal*, Vol. 21 (September, 1968), pp. 349-357; James A. Wilde, "The Expenditure Effects of Grant-in-Aid Programs," *National Tax Journal*, Vol. 21 (September, 1968), pp. 340-348; John C. Weicher, "Aid, Expenditures, and Local Government Structure," *National Tax Journal*, Vol. 25 (December, 1972), pp. 573-583.

[8] Woo Sik Kee, "City-Suburban Differentials in Local Government Fiscal Effort," *National Tax Journal*, Vol. 21 (June, 1968), pp. 183-189.

[9] Bernard H. Booms, "City Governmental Form and Public Expenditure Levels," *National Tax Journal*, Vol. 19, (June, 1966), pp. 187-199.

[10] Oliver P. Williams, "A Typology for Comparative Local Government," *Midwest Journal of Political Science*, Vol. 5 (May, 1961), pp. 150-164.

[11] Terry N. Clark, "Community Structure, Decision-making, Budget Expenditures, and Urban Renewal in 51 American Communities," *American Sociological Review* (August, 1968), pp. 585-587.

[12] Thomas R. Dye, "Urban School Segregation: A Comparative Analysis," *Urban Affairs Quarterly* (December, 1968), pp. 141-165.

[13] Thomas R. Dye, "Governmental Structure, Urban Environment, and Educational Policy," *Midwest Journal of Political Science* (August, 1967), pp. 353-380.

[14] Thomas R. Dye, "City-Suburban Social Distance and Public Policy," *Social Forces* (September, 1965), pp. 100-106.

[15] Brett W. Hawkins, *op. cit.*, p. 83.

[16] Chester B. Rodgers, "Environment, System and Output," *Social Forces* (September, 1969), p. 86.

[17] *Ibid.* p. 85

[18] George S. Duggar, "The Relation of Local Government Structure to Urban Renewal," *Law and Contemporary Problems* (Winter, 1961), pp. 55-65.

[19] Robert L. Crain and Donald B. Rosenthal, Structure and Values in Local Political Systems: The Case of Fluoridation Decisions," *Journal of Politics*, Vol. 28 (February, 1966), pp. 169-195.

[20] Brett W. Hawkins, *op. cit.*, p. 87.

[21] Robert L. Lineberry and Edmund P. Fowler, "Reformism and Public Policy in American Cities," *American Political Science Review*, Vol. 61 (September, 1967), pp. 701-716.

[22] *Ibid.* p. 716.

[23] Michael Aiken and Robert R. Alford, "Community Structure and Innovation: The Case of Public Housing," *American Political Science Review*, Vol. 64 (September, 1970), pp. 843-864; and "Community Structure and Innovation: The Case of Urban Renewal," *American Sociological Review*, Vol. 35 (August, 1970).

[24] Heinz Eulau and Kenneth Prewitt, *Labyrinths of Democracy: Adaptations, Linkages, Representation, and Policies in Urban Politics* (New York: Bobbs-Merrill, 1973); Heinz Eulau and Robert Eyestone, "Policy Maps of City Councils and Policy Outcomes," *American Political Science Review*, Vol. 62 (March, 1968), pp. 124-144; Kenneth Prewitt, *The Recruitment of Political Leaders* (New York: Bobbs-Merrill, 1970); Ronald O. Loveridge, *City Managers in Legislative Politics* (New York: Bobbs-

Merrill, 1972); and Betty H. Zisk, *Local Interest Politics: A One-Way Street* (New York: Bobbs-Merrill, 1973).

[25] Eulau and Prewitt, *op. cit.*, p. 25.

[26] Especially Tables 6-1 and 6-2, pp. 146-149.

Notes to Chapter 4

[1] Robert Salisbury, "The Analysis of Public Policy: The Search for Theories and Roles" in Austin Ranney (ed.) *Political Science and Public Policy* (Chicago: Markham, 1968), 151-178. See also Ire Sharkansky (ed.), *Policy Analysis In Political Science* (Chicago: Markham, 1970).

[2] Path analysis is by no means a new methodology. Sewall Wright published the first article on the topic in 1921, and the method was discussed at length in biology and genetics in the 1920's and 30's. Sewall Wright, "Correlation and Causation," *Journal of Agricultural Research*, Vol. 20 (1921), 557-585; H. E. Niles, "Correlation, Causation, and Wright's Theory of 'Path Coefficients'," *Genetics*, Vol. 7 (1922), 258-273; Sewall Wright, "The Theory of Path Coefficients: A Reply to Niles Criticism," *Genetics*, Vol. 8 (1923), 239-255; H. E. Niles, "The Method of Path Coefficients: An Answer to Wright," *Genetics*, Vol. 8 (1923) 256-260; Sewall Wright, "The Method to Path Coefficients" *Annals of Mathematical Statistics*, Vol. 5 (1934), 161-215; J. W. Tukey, "Causation, Regression and Path Analysis," in Oscar Kempthorne (ed.), *Statistics and Mathematics in Biology* (New York: Hafner Publishing Co., 1954); Sewall Wright, "Path Coefficients and Path Regressions: Alternative or Complementary Concepts" *Biometrics*, Vol. 16 (1960), 180-202; Malcolm E. Turner and Charles D. Stevens, "The Regression Analysis of Causal Paths," *Biometrics*, Vol. 15 (1959), 236-258. Econometricians developed an extensive literature in path analysis and related techniques in the 1950's. See. E. Malinvaud, *Statistical Methods of Econometrics* (Chicago: Rand McNally, 1966). Raymond Boudon recommended path analysis to sociologists in 1965 as an improvement over the Simon-Blalock type of casual modeling, which Boudon labeled as a "weak form" of path analysis. (Boudon refered to

path analysis as "dependence analysis", but "path analysis" seems
to be the more common usage.) Raymond Boudon, "A Method of
Linear Causal Analysis: Dependence Analysis", *American Sociological Review*, Vol. 30 (June, 1965); 365-374. See also Hubert
M. Blalock Jr., *Causal Inferences in Nonexperimental Research*
(Chapel Hill University of North Carolina Press, 1964). Otis
Dudley Duncan also recommended this technique to sociologists
as "useful in making explicit the rationale of conventional regression equations"; he re-analyzed data from several sociological
studies to demonstrate the utility of the method. Otis Dudley
Duncan "Path Analysis: Sociological Examples," *American Journal of Sociology*, Vol. 72 (July, 1966), 1-16. In 1967 H. M. Blalock, Jr. discussed the utility of closed theoretical systems in causal inference (and hence by implication the utility of path analysis) in political science—specifically in the study of constituency
influence in congressional voting behavior. H. M. Blalock, Jr.,
"Causal Inferences, Closed Populations, and Measures of Association," *American Political Science Review*, Vol. 61 (March,
1967), 130-136. Yet policy research, in political science at least,
has not yet moved beyond the Simon-Blalock technique. See
Charles F. Cnudde and Donald J. McCrone, "Party Competition
and Welfare Policies in the American States," *American Political
Science Review*, Vol. 63 (September, 1969), 858-866. Nonetheless,
it is very likely that path analysis will be employed increasingly as
policy researchers seek to develop and test increasingly complex
causal models. See also H. M. Blalock Jr. (ed.), *Causal Models
in the Social Sciences* (New York: Aldine-Atherton, 1971).

[3] The simple correlation coefficients for relationships with po-
licemen per 10,000 for 245 cities are: population size—.36; non-
white population percentage—.47; percent owner-occupied dwelling units— -.48; median family income—.13; crime rate—.48; and
per capita total revenue—.57.

[4] See Terrence Jones, "Evaluating Everyday Policies: Police
Activity and Crime Incidence," *Urban Affairs Quarterly* (March,
1973), pp. 267-279.

[5] Harold Wilensky, *The Welfare State and Equality* (Berkeley:

University of Califorina Press, 1975).
[6] *Ibid.*, pp. 27-28.

Notes to Chapter 5

[1] James S. Coleman, *Equality of Educational Opportunity* (Washington: Government Printing Office, 1966).

[2] U.S. Commission of Civil Rights, *Racial Isolation in the Public Schools*, 2 Vols. (Washington: Government Printing Office, 1967).

[3] David J. Armor, "The Evidence on Busing," *The Public Interest*, No. 28 (Summer, 1972), pp. 90-126.

[4] Thomas F. Pettigrew. et.al., "Busing: A Review of 'The Evidence'", *The Public Interest*, No. 31 (Spring, 1973), pp. 88-113.

[5] David J. Armor, "The Double Double Standard", *The Public Interest*, No 31, (Spring, 1973), pp. 119-131.

[6] Christopher Jencks, *Inequality: A Reassessment of the Effect of Family and Schooling In America* (New York: Basic Books, 1972).

[7] James Q. Wilson, "On Pettigrew and Armor," *The Public Interest*, No. 31 (Spring, 1973), pp. 132-134.

INDEX